100 Hikes in
Central Oregon
CASCADES

William L. Sullivan

Navillus Press
Eugene

FOR GEORGE

William Sullivan

McKenzie River Trail near Tamolitch Dry Falls.

Published by the Navillus Press
1958 Onyx Street
Eugene, Oregon 97403

Printed in USA on Envirotext, 100% recycled paper

Cover: Gentian, Broken Top from a tarn above Golden Lake.
Spine: Jefferson Park
Frontispiece: Fog on the trail to Mt. June

SAFETY CONSIDERATIONS: Many of the trails in this book pass throughWilderness and remote country where hikers are exposed to unavoidable risks. On any hike, the weather may change suddenly. The fact that a hike is included in this book, or that it may be rated as easy, does not necessarily mean it will be safe or easy for you. Prepare yourself with proper equipment and outdoor skills, and you will be able to enjoy these hikes with confidence.

Every effort has been made to assure the accuracy of the information in this book. The author has hiked all 100 of the featured trails, and the trails' administrative agencies have reviewed the maps and text. Nonetheless, construction, logging, and storm damage may cause changes. Corrections and updates are welcome, and may be sent in care of the publisher.

Contents

*R – Crowded or restricted backpacking area

3

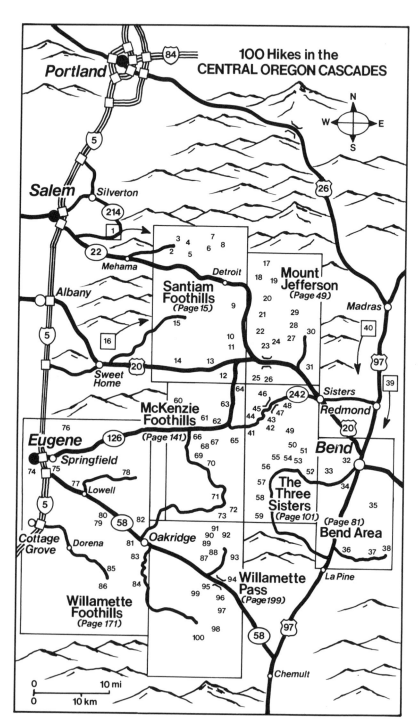

100 Hikes in the
CENTRAL OREGON CASCADES

*R – Crowded or restricted backpacking area

*R – Crowded or restricted backpacking area

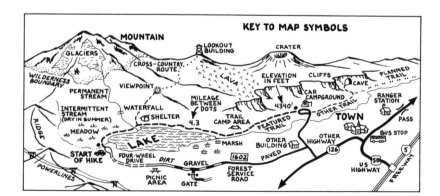

KEY TO MAP SYMBOLS

Introduction

Welcome to Oregon's favorite hiking area, the mountains between the Willamette Valley and Bend. Few regions pack such a variety of trails into an area crossable by a 2-hour drive. This guide covers more than just the well-known Wilderness Areas from Mt. Jefferson to Diamond Peak. You'll discover paths to a waterfall glen near Sweet Home, a cluster of lava caves near Newberry Crater, a natural rock arch near Detroit, a gold-mining ghost town near Cottage Grove, and a riverside oasis near Sunriver. Twenty-one of the trips are open even in winter, when snow blocks the High Cascades.

The book features a variety of difficulty levels. Hikers with children will find 48 hikes carefully chosen for them. As a parent of 2 pre-teens, I understand how enthused children become about chipmunks or splashing creeks, and how curiously uninspired they seem by glorious viewpoints or steep trails. On the other hand, a quarter of the hikes included are unabashedly difficult, with outstanding beauty and challenge. Fifty-one of the trails are rated as suitable for backpackers as well as day hikers. And if you really want to get away from it all, a list at the back of the book briefly describes 100 *more* hikes in the Central Oregon Cascades — little-known but interesting trips for adventurous spirits.

HOW TO USE THIS BOOK

It's Easy to Choose a Trip

The featured hikes are divided into 7 regions, from the Santiam Foothills to Willamette Pass. To choose a trip, simply turn to the area that interests you and look for the following symbols in the upper right-hand corner of each hike's heading. Whether you're hiking with children, backpacking, or looking for a snow-free winter trail, you'll quickly find an outing to match your tastes.

 Children's favorites — walks popular with the 4- to 12-year-old crowd, but fun for hikers of all ages.

 All-year trails, hikable most or all of winter.

 Hikes suitable for backpackers as well as day hikers. No permits required. Crowds unlikely.

 Restricted or crowded backpacking areas. Permits are required in the Mt. Jefferson, Mt. Washington, and Three Sisters Wilderness Areas.

The Information Blocks

Each hike is rated by difficulty. **Easy** hikes are between 2 and 7 miles round-trip and gain less than 1000 feet in elevation. Never very steep nor particularly remote, they make good warm-up trips for experienced hikers or first-time trips for novices.

Trips rated as **Moderate** range from 4 to 11 miles round-trip. Long "moderate" hikes are not steep, but shorter trails may gain up to 2300 feet of elevation — or they may require some pathfinding skills. Hikers must be in good condition and will need to take several rest stops.

Difficult trails demand top physical condition, with a strong heart and strong knees. These challenging hikes are 8 to 15 miles round-trip and may gain 3000 feet or more. Backpacking can break difficult hikes into manageable segments.

Distances are given in round-trip mileage, except for those trails where a car or bicycle shuttle is so convenient that the suggested hike is one-way only, and is listed as such.

Elevation gains tell much about the difficulty of a hike. Those who puff climbing a few flights of stairs may consider even 500 feet of elevation a strenuous climb, and should watch this listing carefully. Note that the figures are for each hike's *cumulative* elevation gain, adding all the uphill portions, even those on the return trip.

The **hiking season** of any trail varies with the weather. In a cold year, a trail described as "Open May through October" may not yet be clear of snow by May 1, and may be socked in by a blizzard before October 31. Similarly, a trail that is "Open all year" may close due to storms.

All hikers should carry a topographic **map,** with contour lines to show elevation. Maps listed as "USFS" are available from U.S. Forest Service offices. Those tagged "USGS" are published by the U.S. Geological Survey and can be found at many outdoor stores. Or you can write to the USGS, PO Box 25286, Denver, CO 80225 to have maps sent postpaid. Indicate that the maps are part of the 7.5-minute series for Oregon. In addition, it pays to pick up a Willamette National Forest Visitor Map (for the west side of the mountains) or a Deschutes National Forest Map (for the east) at a ranger station for a couple dollars.

WILDERNESS RESTRICTIONS

From the last weekend in May to the end of October, permits are required to enter the 3 most popular Wilderness Areas — Mt. Jefferson, Mt. Washington, and the Three Sisters. In most cases you can fill these out at the trailhead, but restrictions are tightening as use increases. In 1996, two trails require advance reservations: the Pamelia Lake Trail (Hike #20) and the Obsidian Trail (Hike #42). In addition, overnight use at 15 popular wilderness lakes is limited to approved campsites designated by a post, and campfires are banned in many heavily used areas. After 1996, backpackers probably will need to pick up a permit in advance to camp in popular areas. Check with a Forest Service office.

Many other restrictions apply to **all** Wilderness Areas, and affect 50 of the hikes featured in this guide:

- Groups must be no larger than 12.
- Campfires are banned within 100 feet of any water source or maintained trail.
- No one may enter areas posted as closed for rehabilitation.
- Bicycles and other wheeled vehicles (except wheelchairs) are banned.
- Horses and pack stock cannot be tethered within 200 feet of any water source or shelter.
- Motorized equipment and fireworks are banned.
- Live trees and shrubs must not be cut or damaged.

North Sister and Middle Sister from tarn near Broken Top.

In addition, some rules apply to all federal lands:

- Collecting arrowheads or other cultural artifacts is a federal crime.
- Permits are required to dig up plants.

SAFETY ON THE TRAIL

Wild Animals

Part of the fun of hiking is watching for wildlife. Lovers of wildness rue the demise of our most impressive species. Wolves and grizzly bears are extinct in Oregon. The little black bears that remain are so profoundly shy you probably won't see one in 1000 miles of hiking. In this portion of the Cascades, the only reason for backpackers to hang their food from a tree at night is to protect it from ground squirrels. Likewise, our rattlesnakes are genuinely rare and shy — and they never were as venomous as the Southwest's famous rattlers.

Ticks have received some publicity as carriers of Lyme disease, which begins with flu-like symptoms and an often circular rash. While this is a problem in the Eastern states, only a couple of cases have been reported in Oregon. Nonetheless, brush off your clothes and check your ankles after walking through dry grass or brush.

Mosquitoes can be a nuisance on hikes in the Mt. Jefferson, Three Sisters, and Willamette Pass sections. To avoid them, remember that these insects hatch about 10 days after the snow melts from the trails and that they remain in force 3 or 4 weeks. Thus, if a given trail in the High Cascades is listed as "Open mid-June," expect mosquitoes there most of July.

Drinking Water

Day hikers should bring all the water they will need — roughly a quart per person. A microscopic paramecium, *Giardia*, has forever changed the old custom of dipping a drink from every brook. The symptoms of "beaver fever," debilitating nausea and diarrhea, commence a week or 2 after ingesting *Giardia*.

If you love fresh water and are willing to gamble, consider that the paramecium is spread only by mammals, enters the water by defecation, and moves only downstream. As a result, gushing springs and runoff immediately below snowfields are less dangerous. If you're backpacking, bring an approved water filter or purification tablet, or boil your water 5 minutes.

Proper Equipment

Even on the tamest hike a surprise storm or a wrong turn can suddenly make the gear you carry very important. Always bring a pack with the 10 essentials:

1. Warm, water-repellent coat (or parka and extra shirt)
2. Drinking water
3. Extra food
4. Knife
5. Matches in waterproof container
6. Fire starter (butane lighter or candle)
7. First aid kit
8. Flashlight
9. Map (topographic, if possible)
10. Compass

Before leaving on a hike, tell someone where you are going so they can alert the county sheriff to begin a search if you do not return on time. If you're lost, stay put and keep warm. The number one killer in the woods is *hypothermia* — being cold and wet too long.

COURTESY ON THE TRAIL

As our trails become more heavily used, rules of trail etiquette become stricter. Please:

- Pick no flowers.
- Leave no litter. Eggshells and orange peels can last for decades.
- Do not bring pets into wilderness areas. Dogs can frighten wildlife and disturb other hikers.
- Step off the trail on the downhill side to let horses pass. Speak to them quietly to help keep them from spooking.
- Do not shortcut switchbacks.

For backpackers, low-impact camping was once merely a courtesy, but is on the verge of becoming a requirement, both to protect the landscape and to preserve a sense of solitude for others. The most important rules:

- Camp out of sight of lakes and trails.
- Build no campfire. Cook on a backpacking stove.
- Wash 100 feet from any lake or stream.
- Camp on duff, rock, or sand — never on meadow vegetation.
- Pack out garbage — don't burn or bury it.

FOR MORE INFORMATION

All major Forest Service offices in the area collect reports of trail conditions in TRIS, a computerized trail information system available to the public. By typing a trail's name or number into a computer terminal at a Forest Service office, you can theoretically access updated information on snow levels, trail maintenance, and new construction. Unfortunately, the information is often sketchy or out of date. Nonetheless, it's a promising beginning, with the laudable goal of eventually cataloguing every trail on public land in the state.

If you'd like to check on a trail, and if TRIS is inconvenient for you, call directly to the trail's administrative agency. These agencies are listed below, along with the hikes in this book for which they manage trails.

Hike	Managing Agency
32	Bend Metro Park and Rec. District — (541) 389-7275
33, 34, 52-59	Bend Ranger District — (541) 388-5664
60, 68-71	Blue River Ranger District — (541) 822-3317
76	Bureau of Land Mgmt., Eugene — (541) 683-6481
85, 86	Cottage Grove Ranger District — (541) 942-5591
94, 96-98	Crescent Ranger District — (541) 433-2234
40	Crooked River Nat'l Grasslands — (541) 447-9640
2-9, 17-23	Detroit Ranger District — (503) 854-3366
74	Eugene Parks — (541) 687-5325
35-38	Fort Rock Ranger District — (541) 388-5674
75, 86	Lane County Parks — (541) 341-6940
16	Linn County Parks — (541) 967-3917
78-82	Lowell Ranger District — (541) 937-2129
25, 26, 41-46, 61-67	McKenzie Ranger District — (541) 822-3381
75	Mount Pisgah Arboretum — (541) 747-3817
72, 73, 87-93, 95, 99	Oakridge Ranger District — (541) 782-2291
83, 84, 100	Rigdon Ranger District — (541) 782-2283
27-31, 47-51	Sisters Ranger District — (541) 549-2111
1, 39, 40, 77	State Parks and Rec. Dept. — (503) 378-6305
10-15	Sweet Home Ranger District — (541) 367-5168

Reflection in Williams Lake.

Santiam Foothills

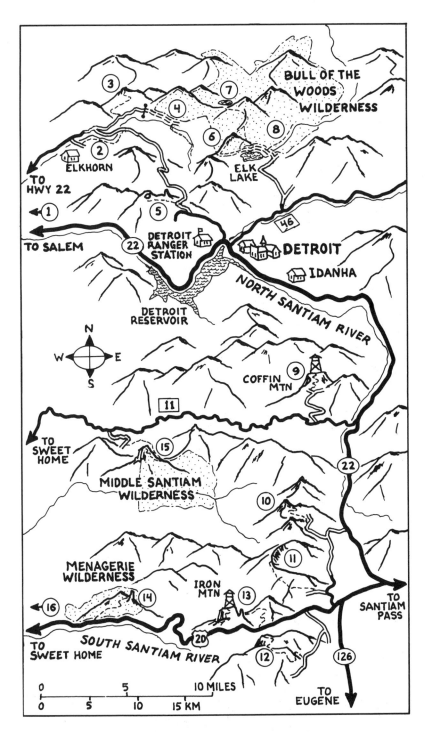

Opposite: *South Falls of Silver Creek (Hike #1).*

1   Silver Creek Falls

Easy
7-mile loop
600 feet elevation gain
Open all year
Map: Drake Crossing (USGS)

This popular hike through Silver Falls State Park's forested canyons visits 10 spectacular waterfalls, 5 more than 100 feet high. The path even leads through mossy caverns *behind* the falls' shimmering silver curtains.

This loop is a good spring conditioner for experienced hikers. Yet it's also suitable for families with beginners, because side trails provide shortcuts back to the car, trimming the total distance to 5.1, 2.4, or just 0.7 miles. The park is usually snow-free even in mid-winter. From May through September, a $4 parking fee is charged throughout the park.

Drive 10 miles east of Salem on Highway 22, turn north at a sign for Silver Falls Park, and follow Highway 214 for 16 miles to the large park entrance sign at South Falls. (Coming from the north, exit Interstate 5 at Woodburn and follow Highway 214 southeast, through Silverton 30 miles to the park.)

When entering the South Falls parking complex, keep to the right for 0.6 mile and park at the last, least crowded lot. At the end of the turnaround, take the trail into the woods and walk left to an overlook of South Falls. From here take the paved trail to the right, switchbacking down into the canyon and behind 177-foot South Falls.

All waterfalls in the park spill over 15-million-year-old Columbia River basalt. As the lava slowly cooled, it sometimes fractured to form the honeycomb of columns visible on cliff edges. Circular indentations in the ceilings of the misty caverns behind the falls are *tree wells*, formed when the lava flows hardened around burning trees. The churning of Silver Creek gouged the soft soil from beneath the harder lava, leaving these caverns and casts.

A few hundred yards beyond South Falls is a junction at a scenic footbridge. Don't cross the bridge; that route merely returns to the car. Instead take the unpaved path along the creek. This route eventually switchbacks down and behind Lower South Falls' broad, 93-foot cascade.

Beyond Lower South Falls the trail forks again. Tired hikers can turn right and climb the steepish ridge trail to the canyon rim and parking lot, for a total of 2.4 miles. If you're ready for a longer hike continue straight, heading up the north fork of Silver Creek to 30-foot Lower North Falls. At a footbridge just above the falls, take a 100-yard side trail to admire tall, thin Double Falls. Then continue on the main trail past Drake and Middle North Falls to the Winter Falls trail junction.

Drake Falls.   Opposite: Maidenhair fern.

Wearing down? Then opt for the 5.1-mile loop by turning right, climbing to Winter Falls, and taking the return trail to the South Falls parking area. Still not tired? Then continue straight on the 7-mile loop, passing Twin Falls and finally hiking behind North Falls' inspiring 136-foot plume. At a junction above North Falls, turn right onto the return trail, which parallels the highway along the canyon rim for 0.9 mile to the Winter Falls parking pullout. At the far end of the pullout the trail continues along the highway, at times meandering into the woods and crossing a paved bike path. When the trail meets the parking lot entrance road, turn right for 0.2 mile to the car.

Other Hiking Options

Crowds are thinner if you start at the North Falls parking area instead. And while there, don't overlook the 0.2-mile side trail which leads under the highway bridge to less-visited Upper North Falls' quiet pool.

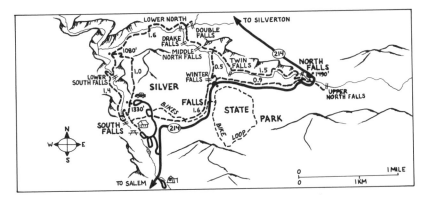

2   Little North Santiam

Moderate
9 miles round-trip
900 feet elevation gain
Open all year
Map: Elkhorn (USGS)

The Little North Santiam has long been known for its swimmable green pools, so tempting on hot summer days. This trail, recently built by Salem volunteers along a less well-known portion of the scenic river's bank, reveals that the river has other charms as well: hidden waterfalls, spring trilliums, and mossy, old-growth forests lit with autumn-reddened vine maple.

To shorten this trip to 4.5 miles bring a second car as a shuttle and hike the trail one-way. To lengthen the trip, bring a backpack; the trail traverses several campable river benches.

To find the lower trailhead, turn north off Highway 22 at the Swiss Village Restaurant in Mehama (23 miles east of Salem). Follow the paved road up the Little North Santiam 14.5 miles, turn right onto a gravel road signed "Elkhorn Drive SE," drive across the river bridge, continue 0.4 mile further, and park on the left at a brown post marking the trailhead.

The trail begins by skirting a tree plantation for 0.2 mile, then plunges into an ancient Douglas fir forest carpeted with sword ferns, vanilla leaf, and shamrock-shaped sourgrass. At the 0.7-mile mark, notice a small waterfall in the river to the left. For a fun detour take a faint side trail to the falls -- a chute with a deep, clear pool and a shoreline of river-rounded bedrock ideal for sunbathing.

Return to the main trail, which now begins climbing steeply to bypass a precipitous narrows in the river canyon. Viewpoints yield glimpses across the

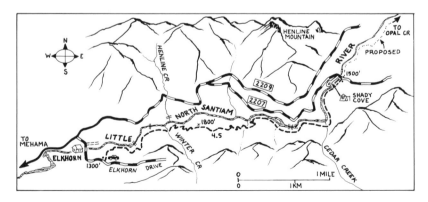

Little North Santiam River.   Opposite: Sourgrass (Oxalis).

canyon to Henline Creek's triple falls and Henline Mountain's cliffs (see Hike #3). The trail switchbacks down to the river again at the 2.3-mile mark and remains relatively level thereafter.

At the 3.3-mile mark, a short side trail to the left leads to a remarkable view of 4 emerald pools separated by small waterfalls. Though the pools are inaccessible here, the trail soon descends within a short scramble of a pebble beach.

The trail reaches gravel Road 2207 at the south end of a historic wooden bridge rebuilt in 1991. To bring a shuttle car to this trailhead, drive up the Little North Santiam Road 1.8 miles past the Elkhorn Drive turnoff (continue 1.3 miles past the end of pavement), and then turn right on Road 2207 for 2 miles.

Other Hiking Options

An additional segment of the Little North Santiam Trail has been proposed for construction. When complete, it will continue 6.1 miles beyond Road 2207 to join the existing trail at Opal Creek (see Hike #4). Backpackers in particular should find this connection tempting.

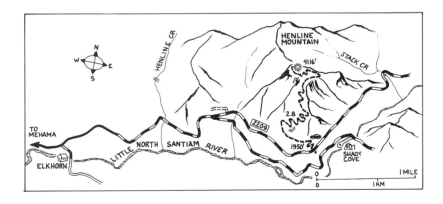

3   Henline Mountain

Moderate
5.6 miles round-trip
2200 feet elevation gain
Open April to mid-November
Map: Elkhorn (USGS)

    This delightful climb, handy for a quick bit of exercise, leads to the site of a lookout tower on the rocky shoulder of Henline Mountain. The tower is gone, but the view is still here, extending beyond the Little North Santiam's forest-rimmed valley to Mount Jefferson.

    To find the trailhead, turn north off Highway 22 at the Swiss Village Restaurant in Mehama (23 miles east of Salem), follow the paved Little North Santiam Road for 15 miles, and continue straight on gravel for another 1.3 miles to a fork. Veer left on Road 2209 past the sign "Road Closed 6 Miles Ahead." Precisely 1.0 mile past this fork — watch the odometer! — look sharply for a hiker-symbol sign on a steep, unlikely-looking roadcut to the left. Park on the shoulder here.

    The trail climbs up the roadcut, switchbacks several times in the forest (enlivened by rhododendron blooms in June), and traverses a large rockslide. At 0.7 mile, after another switchback, take a short side trail to the right to a rock outcropping. The view here overlooks both the rockslide and the Little North Santiam Valley.

    The trail climbs steadily to the 2-mile mark, where it briefly levels to traverse a ridge to the right toward another viewpoint, this one with a first glimpse of Mt. Jefferson's snowy summit. Shortly thereafter, the trails grows rockier and switchbacks up more steeply. Just 0.3 mile from the top, take a breather at a viewpoint by an interesting rock pinnacle on the left. Then continue on to the trail's end atop a rocky ridge inhabited by a few struggling manzanita bushes. Though the actual summit of Henline Mountain is a mile north and 530 feet higher, the lookout tower was built on this more visible knoll. Small bolts and bits of broken glass mark the site.

The snowless, square-topped mountain on the eastern horizon is Battle Ax (see Hike #6). To the west, try to spot the golf course at Elkhorn and, on a clear day, Marys Peak in the Coast Range 65 miles away.

Elkhorn Mountain from Henline Trail.   *Opposite: Vine maple.*

4   Opal Creek

Easy (to Opal Pool)
7 miles round-trip
200 feet elevation gain
Open all year
Maps: Battle Ax, Elkhorn (USGS)

Moderate (to Beachie Creek)
10.4 miles round-trip
500 feet elevation gain

Opal Creek's ancient forest, on the edge of the Bull of the Woods Wilderness, was thrust to fame in the 1980s by controversy over Forest Service logging proposals. National television crews and thousands of visitors hiked to Jawbone Flats' rustic mining camp and scrambled over a rugged "bear trail" to view the old-growth groves towering above this creek's small waterfalls and green pools.

Although Opal Creek is still not officially protected, an improved path has been built to make the area more hiker-friendly. The new trail shortcuts from the Little North Santiam River to Opal Creek, bypassing Jawbone Flats.

Start by driving Highway 22 to Mehama (23 miles east of Salem). Turn north at the sign for Elkhorn, follow the paved Little North Santiam Road for 15 miles, and continue straight on gravel for another 1.3 miles to a fork. Veer left on Road 2209 past the sign "Road Closed 6 Miles Ahead" and drive to the locked gate. Residents of Jawbone Flats are allowed to drive the dirt road ahead; others must park and walk.

The pleasantly primitive road crosses Gold Creek on a 60-foot-high bridge, skirts dramatic cliffs above the Little North Santiam River, and winds through an old-growth grove as impressive as any found further upstream.

At the 2-mile mark, stop to inspect the rusting machinery of Merten Mill on the right. The mill operated briefly during the Depression, using winches from the battleship *USS Oregon,* but folded after 2 of the mill's lumber trucks fell off

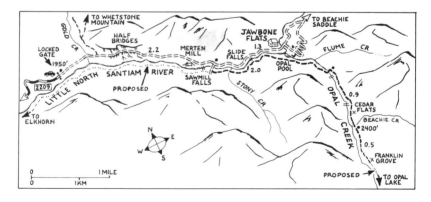

the narrow canyon road. Now a recommended camping area for backpackers, the mill site has one small empty building that can serve as emergency shelter. A short side trail behind the building leads to Sawmill Falls, a 30-foot cascade pouring into a deep green pool ideal for swimming.

The road forks 0.2 mile beyond Merten Mill, offering 2 options. Day hikers interested in the area's mining history may wish to continue straight on the main road 1.1 mile to Jawbone Flats, a well-preserved collection of 27 buildings dating from 1929-1932. Jawbone Flats was donated to the Nature Conservancy in 1993 as an old-growth reserach center. Respect the residents' privacy by staying on the road. Cross a bridge, turn right at a building with a humming water-power generator, and walk 0.2 mile further to a sign indicating a short side trail to Opal Pool's scenic gorge — a rewarding goal for an easy hike.

If you're headed for the trail up Opal Creek, however, don't go to Jawbone Flats. Instead, turn right at the road fork beyond Merten Mill, cross the river on an old log bridge, and turn left onto the Opal Creek Trail. The path follows the Little North Santiam River a mile, crosses a forested bench to an overlook of Opal Pool, and then ascends Opal Creek about 3 miles, passing several small waterfalls and Cedar Flat's trio of 1000-year-old red cedars. The Beachie Creek crossing, on a mossy log, makes a good stopping point.

Sawmill Falls.   Opposite: Old-growth forest near Merten Mill.

5   Phantom Bridge

Moderate
5.4 miles round-trip
1400 feet cumulative elevation gain
Open late June to mid-November
Map: Battle Ax (USGS)

This natural rock arch, hidden alongside a ridgetop cliff between Detroit and the Bull of the Woods Wilderness, spans a 50-foot chasm, yet is solid enough that some daring souls creep to its middle. The hike along the ridge to the arch is admittedly rough in spots, but the route compensates with avalanche lilies, huckleberries, and views of the High Cascades from Mt. Hood to the Three Sisters.

Start by driving to Detroit on Highway 22. Immediately west of town, at the west end of the Breitenbush River Arm bridge, turn north onto French Creek Road (#2223). Follow this paved, one-lane road 4.1 miles and turn right onto gravel Road 2207 for 3.7 miles. Just before a saddle, watch for a hiker-symbol sign at the trailhead on the left. Park at a turnout 100 feet further and walk back to the trail.

The trail begins in an old clearcut, but soon heads left around a wooded hill. At the 0.6-mile mark, cross a saddle and traverse to the right, through a rockslide at the base of Dog Rock's monolith. The trail returns to the ridgecrest amid masses of white avalanche lilies (in late June) and huckleberries (in late August). A small rocky knoll to the right has a particularly fine view of Opal Lake and a dozen notable peaks, including Battle Ax (Hike #6), Mt. Jefferson, and square-topped Coffin Mountain (Hike #9).

The trail then descends steeply to Cedar Lake. After passing this small pond,

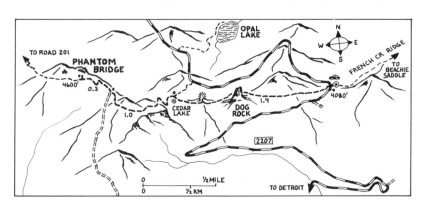

Phantom Bridge.   Opposite: Avalanche lilies.

continue along the ridge, switchbacking up to a small summit and then dipping to an open plateau. Follow cairns across this highland, then descend through a clearcut, cross a gravel logging road turnaround, and climb the ridge 0.3 mile further to a "Phantom Bridge" sign pointing to the right. A 50-foot scramble to the ridgecrest finally reveals the arch.

Mt. Jefferson and Elk Lake from Battle Ax.   Opposite: Cat's ear.

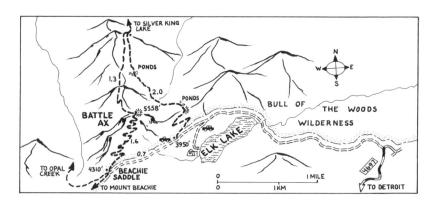

6   Battle Ax

Moderate
5.6-mile loop
1600 feet elevation gain
Open mid-June through October
Map: Bull of the Woods Wilderness
    (USFS)

Tallest peak in the Bull of the Woods Wilderness, Battle Ax not only commands views from Mt. Hood to Diamond Peak, it also hosts an interesting rock garden of subalpine wildflowers and weather-stunted trees. The loop trail to the summit returns around the mountain's base, past a collection of tranquil ponds. The mountain gets its name either from the peak's sharp, hatchet-shaped silhouette, or else from a brand of chewing tobacco popular when gold prospectors scoured this area in the 1890s.

Drive to this hike by turning off Highway 22 in Detroit at the sign for Breitenbush River. Follow paved Road 46 north for 4.4 miles and turn left onto gravel Road 4696 at a small sign for Elk Lake. Turn left again in 0.8 mile onto Road 4697 at the sign "Elk Road Not Maintained For Trailer Travel." After 4.7 miles of good but steep gravel, turn left at a sign for Elk Lake.

Here the road abruptly worsens. Though level, the track has big potholes and buried boulders that slow travel to a crawl. After 2 miles of this agony, reach the far end of the lake. Passengers cars should probably park here, at the fork to the Elk Lake Campground. More rugged vehicles may drive up the right-hand fork 0.4 mile to a sign for the Bagby Hot Springs Trail. Parking is tight but possible on the shoulder 100 yards beyond the sign.

From whichever place you park, walk on up the road to its end at Beachie Saddle. Then turn right and take the trail up the ridge, switchbacking amid trees dwarfed by winter winds. Watch for huckleberries, strawberry blooms, red Indian paintbrush, and fuzzy cat's ears.

At the summit, only foundation piers remain of the erstwhile fire lookout tower. Take a short side trip out a shaley ridge to the east for a breathtaking view down to Elk Lake.

To continue the loop, return to the lookout site and follow a faint trail along a ridge to the north. After 0.7 mile the trail leaves the ridgecrest and descends through a hemlock forest 0.6 mile to the Bagby Hot Springs Trail. Turn right.

The route now contours across several large rockslides with views of Mt. Jefferson. Listen here for the *meep!* of pikas, the little, round-eared "rock rabbits" inhabiting these rockfalls. Cross a small bridge between 2 lovely lakelets and then pass a spring-watered slope decorated with yellow fawn lilies. After one last viewpoint — this one across Elk Lake — the trail switchbacks down through the forest to the road.

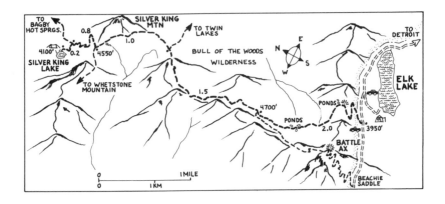

7   Silver King Lake

Difficult
11 miles round-trip
2200 feet cumulative elevation gain
Open June through October
Map: Bull of the Woods Wilderness (USFS)

A ridge extends through the Bull of the Woods Wilderness from Battle Ax to Silver King Mountain, where a quiet lake nestles in a ridge-end niche. This hike balances along the ridgecrest, with views to Mt. Jefferson in the east and Jawbone Flats in the west.

To find the trailhead, turn north off Highway 22 in Detroit at the sign for Breitenbush River. Follow paved Road 46 north for 4.4 miles and turn left onto gravel Road 4696 at a small sign for Elk Lake. Turn left again in 0.8 mile onto Road 4697 at the sign "Elk Road Not Maintained For Trailer Travel." After 4.7 miles of good but steep gravel, turn left at a sign for Elk Lake.

From here on, the road is riddled with big potholes and buried boulders. After 2 frustratingly slow miles, reach the far end of the lake. Passengers cars should probably park here, at the fork to the Elk Lake Campground. Others may drive up the rugged right-hand fork 0.4 mile to the trailhead itself, at a sign for the Bagby Hot Springs Trail. Parking is tight but possible on the shoulder 100 yards beyond the sign.

The trail begins with 2 long switchbacks, climbing steadily through an old-growth forest. White wildflowers predominate in such dark woods; watch for bunchberry and queen's cup. At 0.8 mile, the trail rounds a corner with a wonderful view across Elk Lake to Mt. Jefferson. Then the path levels, contouring about the base of Battle Ax past froggy lakelets and sunny rockslides.

After 2.5 miles the Bagby Hot Springs Trail reaches the ridgecrest, following it with a few ups and downs for 1 mile to a forested saddle and a junction with the Twin Lakes Trail. Stay left toward Bagby.

Next the trail contours around the side of Silver King Mountain for 1 mile. This portion is a little overgrown with beargrass, rhododendron, and huckleberry. Toward the end of this sunny traverse is a small but welcome spring.

Finally reach a small meadow at a pass. Make a sharp switchback to the right to find the trail descending the north side of the pass. Follow this path downhill 0.8 mile, cross a clearing at the foot of a large rockslide, and immediately look for a small sign on a tree indicating the left-hand turnoff to Silver King Lake. Take this side trail uphill 0.2 mile to a lakeside campsite with a picnic table. Mosquitoes are a problem at the lake from mid-June to mid-July. Dense rhododendrons make it difficult but not impossible to walk around the lakeshore for a view of Silver King Mountain.

Other Hiking Options

Twin Lakes provide an alternate goal of about the same difficulty. At the trail junction 3.5 miles along the Bagby Hot Springs Trail, turn right. The trail descends 1.9 miles, dropping 650 feet, to Upper Twin Lake, with the lower twin 0.8 mile beyond.

Hikers with extra energy can return from either destination via the panoramic summit of Battle Ax (see Hike #6), adding 1.6 tough miles.

Silver King Lake.   Opposite: Townsend's chipmunk.

8   Battle Creek

Moderate
8 miles round-trip
900 feet elevation loss
Open mid-May to mid-November
Map: Bull of the Woods Wilderness (USFS)

Here's a switch: this hike begins at a mountain lake and goes *down* to a lowland forest. At the bottom, two large creeks collide, providing plenty of gravel bars and forested benches to explore. Battle Creek is also a jumping-off point for backpackers headed deeper into the Bull of the Woods Wilderness.

Turn north off Highway 22 in Detroit at the sign for Breitenbush River, follow paved Road 46 north for 4.4 miles, and turn left onto gravel Road 4696 at a small sign for Elk Lake. Turn left again in 0.8 mile onto Road 4697 for 4.7 steep miles, and then, at a sign for Elk Lake, turn left onto a horribly rocky, potholed dirt track for 1.4 miles. At the first glimpse of Elk Lake — where the road crosses Elk Lake's outlet creek — park at an unmarked pullout on the right. Then walk 150 yards further along the road to the trailhead, feebly identified by an orange sign on the right with a large black X.

Down the trail 100 yards is the only boggy spot on the entire hike, yet it's soupy enough that tennis shoes won't do. After this the path is better behaved, leading through a forest of old-growth giants for 1.7 almost perfectly level miles. Among the 6-foot-thick hemlock watch for huckleberries, vanilla leaf, and the broad, spiny leaves of devil's club.

The middle third of the 4-mile route is still fairly level, traversing a steep slope with glimpses across Elk Lake Creek's forested canyon. Rhododendrons along this section bloom nicely in June. The last third of the trail descends steadily, losing 800 feet which must, of course, be regained on the trip back.

Finally enter a large, forested flat area with a 4-way trail junction beside the flattened ruin of the former Battle Creek Shelter. Before settling down to lunch, it's fun to explore the area by scouting the various trails.

The trail to the right promptly descends to Elk Lake Creek, which is crossable on logs and stones. The trail straight ahead continues 0.2 mile through a lovely mossy woods to a peninsula, where it crosses Battle Creek on a huge log and heads downstream towards the Welcome Lakes Trail and points east. The trail to the left leads 0.1 mile to a cold ford of Battle Creek, after which it climbs towards the Bull of the Woods lookout via either the Mother Lode or Geronimo trails.

Other Hiking Options

Battle Creek is a good first night's camp for 2- to 4-day backpacking loops . One route is to hike down Elk Lake Creek to the Welcome Lakes Trail, climb to

Old-growth woods near 4-way trail junction.   Opposite: Rhododendron.

the lakes, and return by the Geronimo Trail. Another plan is to head up the Mother Lode Trail to Twin Lakes and return to Elk Lake the following day via Battle Ax (see Hike #7). The Bull of the Woods lookout tower, staffed in times of fire danger, is yet another popular goal.

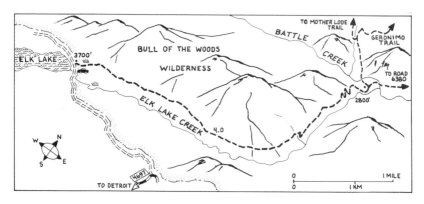

Lookout building with Three Fingered Jack on horizon.   Opposite: Beargrass.

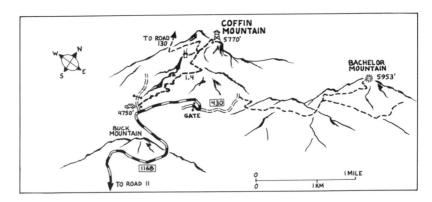

9   Coffin Mountain Lookout

Moderate
2.8 miles round-trip
1000 feet elevation gain
Open late June through October
Map: Coffin Mountain (USGS)

Coffin Mountain's square-topped silhouette seems to be on the horizon wherever one goes in the western Cascade foothills. Towering cliffs make the summit appear unreachable. Yet those who actually visit the peak discover a surprisingly well-graded trail climbing to the lookout tower through a meadow of cheerful wildflower blooms. Along the way, a string of snowy High Cascade peaks is constantly in view.

Turn west off Highway 22 at the sign for Straight Creek Road (2.9 miles east of Marion Forks or 12.6 miles west of the Santiam Y highway junction). Follow the paved Straight Creek Road 4.2 miles, turn right at a sign for the Coffin Mountain Trailhead, drive 3.8 miles up a gravel road, and, following another trailhead sign, drive 100 feet on a spur road to the left to the parking area. Remember to pack extra water for this thirsty hike, since the lookout staff cannot share their limited drinking supply.

The trail starts on an old bulldozer track. After 200 yards turn left onto a friendlier hiking path. Wildflowers are profuse here in early summer. Expect iris, paintbrush, strawberries, larkspur, cat's ears, penstemon, and violets. To the east, Mt. Jefferson rises apparently at arm's length. The view to the west is even more striking: ridge upon desolate ridge of clearcut National Forest, hidden here in the hills behind Detroit Reservoir.

After 0.9 mile begin two long switchbacks across a vast meadow of beargrass. This lily family member blooms in cycles; about every third July the hillside erupts with stalks of white flowers.

Upon reaching the mountain's summit ridgecrest ignore the communications building to the left and instead head right for 0.2 mile, through the trees to the fire lookout. This lonely 16-foot-square outpost becomes a miniature home each summer, with a tiny, stocked kitchen, a visitor's register, and all the books one never had time to read: *Alaska, Little Women, Spanish Through Pictures,* and once, *Is This Where I Was Going?*

Other Hiking Options

If Coffin Mountain's view seems unequaled, try scaling the peak's fraternal twin, nearby Bachelor Mountain. It's a trifle taller but more rounded and less cliffy. Drive 0.7 mile past Coffin Mountain on Road 1168 and turn left on rugged Road 430 for 0.5 mile to its end. The trail climbs past white snags left by the 1970s' Buck Mountain Burn. It's 2 miles to the top and 1100 feet up.

10 The Three Pyramids

Moderate
4.2 miles round-trip
1800 feet elevation gain
Open late June through October
Maps: Echo Mtn., Coffin Mtn. (USGS)

Like a smaller version of the Three Sisters, this trio of ancient volcanic plugs rises in a dramatic cluster above the Old Cascades. To be sure, the Three Pyramids are only half as tall as the more famous mountain triplets, and are not draped with glaciers. But pretty, U-shaped glacial valleys remain from the Ice Age. Today, a short but strenuous trail ascends one of these meadowed valleys, switchbacks up a ridge spangled with alpine wildflowers, and climbs to a former lookout tower site — front row center for a view of High Cascade snowpeaks from Mt. Hood to Diamond Peak.

To reach the trailhead, drive Highway 22 west from the Santiam Y junction for 4.8 miles and turn left onto gravel Road 2067. (Coming from Salem, drive 10.7 miles past Marion Forks and turn right.) After crossing a creek at the 1.9-mile mark of Road 2067, turn right at a sign for the Pyramids Trail and follow Road 560 tenaciously for 3.5 miles. Park at a hiker-symbol sign on the left.

Cross the creek on stepping stones and follow the trail up through a cool, shady old-growth forest. Watch for white woodland wildflowers: vanilla leaf, bunchberry, and delicate star-flowered smilacina. One switchback overlooks a small double cascade in the creek below.

After half a mile's steady climb, cross the creek on stones and climb through a brushy meadow with bracken fern, bleeding hearts, columbine, and false hellebore. At 0.7 mile the trail abruptly turns up the ridge, switchbacking steeply.

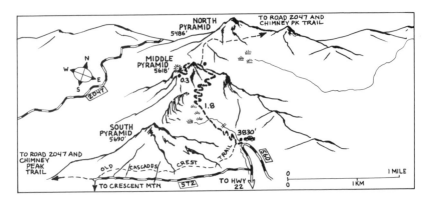

Views now improve to cliffs across the valley and beyond to the Three Sisters.

After 1.5 miles, crest the ridge and traverse behind the north side of Middle Pyramid — a shady slope where snow and trilliums linger into July. Here the views of Mt. Jefferson begin.

The trail winds around to the west face of Middle Pyramid, then switchbacks up to a rocky saddle. The trail appears to end here, between Middle Pyramid's two summits. But the path actually clambers up some rocks to the right and continues 100 yards to the lookout tower site surrounded by cliffs. Almost the entire route of the hike is visible below. To the southwest, note Iron Mountain's distinctive rock thumb. In the west, the rock monolith rising from the Middle Santiam Wilderness' forests is Chimney Peak, with a stripe of Willamette Valley beyond.

Other Hiking Options

The 27-mile Old Cascades Crest Trail, completed in 1995, connects this trail with Crescent Mountain (Hike #11) to the south and Chimney Peak (Hike #15) to the west, opening possibilities for longer shuttle hikes and backpacking trips.

Middle Pyramid's north summit.   Opposite: Star-flowered smilicina.

11   Crescent Mountain

Difficult
8 miles round-trip
2200 feet elevation gain
Open June through October
Map: Echo Mountain (USGS)

Sunny wildflower meadows drape the southern slopes of this huge, crescent-shaped ridge. As the trail angles up through the open fields, expect dramatic views across the High Cascade forests to Mt. Washington and the Three Sisters.

To start the hike, drive half a mile west on Highway 20 from the junction with Highway 126. (Coming from Sweet Home, drive 7.1 miles east of Tombstone Pass.) Turn north onto paved Lava Lake Road at the sign for the Crescent Mountain Trail. After 1 mile turn left onto gravel Road 508 for 0.7 mile to the trailhead pullout on the right.

The trail descends very gradually for its first 1.2 miles to a footbridge across lovely, 8-foot-wide Maude Creek. A small meadow on the far shore makes a nice day-hike goal for children.

After Maude Creek, the trail starts to climb. At the 2.3-mile mark it emerges from the dark woods into a steep meadow of bracken fern and blue lupine. Views open up of snowpeaks to the southeast. Soon, enter a much larger meadow. In early summer the bracken and bunchgrass grow so densely here they sometimes hide the tread.

At the 3.2-mile mark, the trail enters a weather-gnarled stand of mountain hemlock and subalpine fir and then clings to a forested ridgecrest all the way to the top.

Only the wooden floor of the old fire lookout tower survives. From the

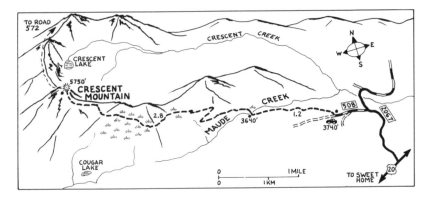

Mt. Washington from Crescent Mountain's meadows.   Opposite: Bracken.

northern edge of the summit look down a cliff to Crescent Lake, curled within the curving mountain's embrace.

Other Hiking Options

   Backpackers or equestrians can continue beyond the summit on the Old Cascades Crest Trail, completed in 1995. The path drops 3 miles to spur Road 572, where the trail forks. Turn west to descend 4 miles along South Pyramid Creek to the Chimney Peak Trail (see Hike #15). Or turn east 1.7 miles to the Three Pyramids Trail (Hike #10) and a longer route to the Chimney Peak Trail.

Cat's ears in summit meadow.   Below: False hellebore leaves.

12   Browder Ridge

Moderate (to viewpoint)
2.8 miles round-trip
1200 feet elevation gain
Open June to mid-November
Maps: Tamolitch Falls, Echo Mtn. (USGS)

Difficult (to summit)
8.4 miles round-trip
2100 feet elevation gain

Browder Ridge, like many of its better-known neighbor peaks in the Old Cascades, sports steep wildflower meadows on its high southern slopes. But no crowds roam Browder Ridge's meadows, as they do at nearby Iron Mountain (Hike #13). And Browder Ridge's view of the High Cascades snowpeaks is second to none.

The trip provides two options: either climb the well-maintained Gate Creek Trail only as far as the viewpoint on the shoulder of Browder Ridge, or venture onward to the ridge's summit via a less well-maintained path and a cross-country meadow route.

To find the Gate Creek Trailhead, drive Highway 20 for 2.3 miles west of the junction with Highway 126 (or 5.3 miles east of Tombstone Pass) and turn south onto Hackleman Creek Road. After 1.7 miles, turn right onto gravel Road 1598 for 2.8 miles to the well-marked trailhead.

The Gate Creek Trail abandons Gate Creek forever after a few yards and instead switchbacks steadily up a forested slope toward Browder Ridge. After 0.4 mile, level out in a stand of 5-foot-thick Douglas fir. Then, at the 1-mile mark, begin climbing steeply up a large meadow of bracken fern, blue mertensia, red columbine, and delicate white star-flowered smilacina. The bracken-covered path climbs up the meadow and into the forest on the right.

After a switchback in the forest, return to the meadow at a glorious viewpoint that makes a worthy goal for a moderate day hike. Here are views of Three Fingered Jack, Mt. Washington, and the Three Sisters. Rock-garden wildflowers cluster at one's feet: showy penstemon, cat's ears, and yellow monkeyflower.

If you're going to the summit, follow the now-level trail west along the ridgecrest. The path grows faint at times in meadows on the left side of the ridgecrest; always keep to the top of the meadows. Beyond the viewpoint 1.7 miles, at the far, upper end of a large meadow, the trail reenters the forest and immediately forks. Turn uphill to the right.

This portion of the trail is poorly maintained, with a few downed logs to step over. Follow the faint trail as it gradually ascends a broad, forested ridge for 0.4 mile to the base of a 150-foot-tall rock cliff. Then the path turns sharply right and traverses a large, steep meadow for 0.5 mile. Just before reentering the forest at a ridgecrest, climb cross-country up the steep meadow, following the ridge to the summit -- a rounded knoll carpeted with heather, phlox, and cat's ears. The 360-degree view encompasses Mt. Jefferson, the South Santiam Canyon, and the entire route of the hike.

Other Hiking Options

Adventurers can follow the Browder Ridge Trail west 3.7 miles from the trail junction at elevation 5200 feet. This route can be hard to find in meadows. It finally descends to Road 080 at a trailhead just a few hundred yards from paved Road 15.

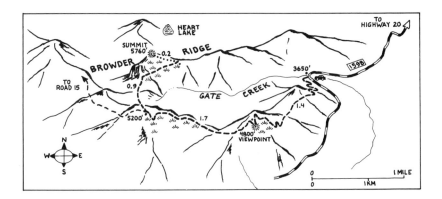

13   Iron Mountain

Easy (to Cone Peak meadows)
3.6 miles round-trip
800 feet elevation gain
Open mid-May to mid-November
Map: Harter Mountain (USGS)

Moderate (to Iron Mountain)
8 miles round-trip
Open mid-June through October
1800 feet elevation gain

Iron Mountain's lookout building is one of the Old Cascades' most popular hiking goals, but most people hike to it the wrong way — up a steep, dusty, largely viewless forest trail on the west side of Tombstone Pass. To really see the July wildflowers that make this area famous, take the longer, better graded Cone Peak Trail through the alpine meadows on the east side of Tombstone Pass. In fact, the viewpoint amid these flower-packed fields makes a worthwhile day-hike destination in itself.

Drive Highway 20 to a shoulder pullout 0.7 mile east of Tombstone Pass and park at the sign, "No Parking for Unattended Vehicles Nov. 15 to Apr. 30," a warning aimed at winter sno-park violators, not hikers.

As the Cone Peak Trail climbs steadily through an old-growth forest watch for shaggy-barked Alaska cedars, rare elsewhere but common here. The entire ridge from Iron Mountain to Echo Mountain is a biological wonderland, featuring more types of trees (17) than any other area in Oregon, and fully 60 plant species considered rare or unusual in the Western Cascades. After 1.1 mile and several switchbacks, emerge from the forests in a rock garden of early-summer wildflowers: fuzzy cat's ears, purple larkspur, yellow stonecrop, and pink penstemon. The path continues across a cinder-strewn shoulder of Cone Peak — a landscape where one wouldn't think plants could grow at all, but where

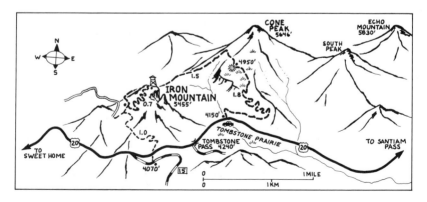

Indian paintbrush and other flowers wash the slopes with color. The viewpoint here overlooks Iron Mountain and Tombstone Prairie.

Beyond the meadow viewpoint the trail descends slightly through forest, crosses a saddle to the north side of Iron Mountain, and contours halfway around the peak to a junction with the Iron Mountain Trail. Turn left and climb 0.7 mile on steep switchbacks to the staffed lookout building. To the east, all the major Cascade peaks are visible; to the west, look for Rooster Rock (Hike #14) and, on a clear day, Marys Peak in the Coast Range.

Be cautious near the summit cliffs. A lookout staffer fell to his death here in 1990. The entire building blew off the peak in a 1976 winter storm and had to be returned by helicopter.

Other Hiking Options

If you arrange a car shuttle between the Cone Peak and Iron Mountain trailheads you can hike both trails in a single 5.7-mile walk. Note that the Iron Mountain Trailhead has been moved away from Highway 20 for safety reasons. To find it, drive 0.5 mile west of Tombstone Pass on the highway and turn south onto Deer Creek Road (Road 15) for 0.3 mile.

Want to hike both trails but can't arrange a shuttle? Then have a designated driver fetch the car. From the Iron Mountain Trail's crossing of Highway 20 it's only 0.7 mile along the highway to the Cone Peak Trailhead.

Iron Mountain from Cone Peak Trail.   Opposite: Stonecrop.

14   Rooster Rock

Moderate
6.4 miles round-trip
2300 feet elevation gain
Open April through November
Map: Menagerie Wilderness (USFS)

Turkey Monster, Rabbit Ears, Chicken Rock — the rock pillars and arches rising from the forests of the Menagerie Wilderness suggest a petrified zoo. In fact, the crags are remnant plugs of the volcanoes that built this portion of the Old Cascades 25 million years ago.

Today, the trail up to Rooster Rock's former lookout site offers not only a look at this ancient menagerie but also a view of the entire South Santiam Canyon from Iron Mountain to the Willamette Valley. The trail is a particularly good choice for a conditioning hike in spring, when the rhododendrons bloom.

Take Highway 20 east of Sweet Home for 21 miles. A few hundred yards east of the Trout Creek Campground entrance, park at a well-marked pullout on the highway's north shoulder. The Trout Creek Trail (#3405) climbs from here toward Rooster Rock at a remarkably steady grade, traversing the hillside without switchbacks. The Douglas fir forest hosts Oregon grape, salal, mossy vine maple, and crowds of May-blooming rhodies. After 2.2 miles the forest briefly opens, offering a view across a valley to Rooster Rock's spire.

At the 2.8-mile mark, join the Rooster Rock Trail (#3399) and begin climbing a little more steeply through a drier forest of madrone, chinkapin, and manzanita. After two quick switchbacks the trail passes the upper base of Rooster Rock and turns left. Uphill 500 yards the trail forks. Ignore the route straight ahead — it's a rough climbers' trail to a logging road near Rabbit Ears' twin

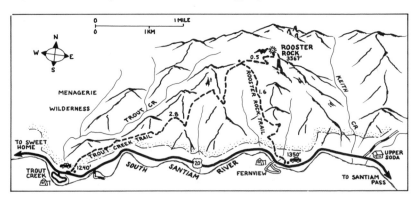

Rabbit Ears. Opposite: Rooster Rock's viewpoint.

260-foot spires. Take the right-hand fork, which promptly leads to an excellent viewpoint atop a bare rock knoll. For years this was the site of a base cabin for a tiny fire lookout shack precariously perched atop Rooster Rock's pinnacle. Only scattered boards remain of the two cabins.

Other Hiking Options

For variety, return via the Rooster Rock Trail, #3399. Though somewhat steeper, this route is very well maintained and over a mile shorter than the Trout Creek route. The two trailheads are 2.5 miles apart on Highway 20 — an unpleasant roadside walk, but a delightful bicycle ride if you've had the foresight to stash a pair of wheels nearby.

15   Chimney Peak

Difficult
12.2 miles round-trip
2300 feet elevation gain
Open mid-June to mid-November
Maps: Quartzville, Chimney Pk. (USGS)

The former lookout site atop this ancient volcanic plug's rocky summit offers a rare look across the Middle Santiam Wilderness, a preserve of towering old-growth forest hidden just 30 miles from the Willamette Valley. Though the trail to the top climbs relentlessly for more than 6 miles, the grade is reasonable and the McQuade Creek Shelter, at the 5-mile mark, provides a welcome rest stop or campsite. Only the last 100 yards to the peak's summit are genuinely difficult; skillfull scrambling is required.

Drive Highway 20 east of Sweet Home 4 miles and turn north at the sign for Quartzville. After following this paved, winding road 24.7 miles, cross a bridge to a 3-way fork in the road. Keep right on paved, one-lane Road 11 for 2.6 miles, turn right onto gravel Road 1142, and climb this winding, narrow route 4 miles to the McQuade Creek Trail sign. Parking is tight but possible on the shoulder of Road 1142; only 4-wheel-drive vehicles should venture to the actual trailhead, 200 yards down a rugged spur road to the left.

In its first half mile the trail crosses 2 forks of McQuade Creek — both bridgeless, but shallow enough that good hiking boots will keep feet dry. Then the trail briefly crosses a ghastly 1989 clearcut and settles down to business: a long, gradual traverse through a steep Douglas fir forest. Twinflower and moss form a carpet here, and rhododendrons paint the trailside pink each June.

At 1.4, 2.6, and 3.9 miles the path curves around major ridge-ends. The last of these corners has a view up Gregg Creek's valley toward Chimney Peak. Just 0.3 mile before reaching the shelter, the trail crosses several creeklets at the head of Gregg Creek. For about 100 yards the tread is overgrown with scrub alder and devil's club, but continue without a switchback and the trail again becomes clear.

Three-walled, tilting McQuade Creek Shelter is 50 feet to the right of the trail. Past the shelter 100 yards, the trail switchbacks to the right and climbs to an unsigned trail junction at a saddle. Go up the ridge to the right. This path makes up for the viewless forests below by offering vistas at every turn. Beyond the saddle 0.7 the trail abruptly ends below a cliffy slope. This was as far as the lookouts' packhorses could climb, and it is the turning-back point for many hikers as well. Now that lookouts' stairs are gone, hikers attempting the dangerous, 100-yard climb to the top must use extreme caution and both hands.

Though the lookout tower was burned, an interesting assortment of forks,

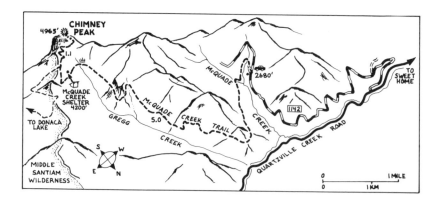

latches, and melted glass lumps remain — all federally protected artifacts that must be left in place.

Other Hiking Options

Backpackers can turn left at the trail junction at the saddle above McQuade Creek Shelter and follow the Chimney Peak Trail 5.5 miles to Donaca Lake. The trail forks a mile beyond the lake at the start of a vast, 23-mile loop around the headwaters of the Middle Santiam River on the Old Cascades Crest Trail. Completed in 1995, this loop crosses the Three Pyramids (Hike #10) and connects with the Crescent Mountain Trail (Hike #11).

McQuade Creek Shelter.   Opposite: Remnants of the burned lookout.

16   McDowell Creek Falls

Easy
1.7-mile loop
200 feet elevation gain
Open all year
Map: Sweet Home (USGS)

This charming glen's 3 lovely waterfalls, low-elevation forest, and easy graveled paths make it ideal for family outings and Sunday strolls. Tucked in a valley near Sweet Home, this little-known miniature version of Silver Creek Falls is hikable all year long.

To drive here from the west, take Highway 20 past Lebanon 4 miles, turn left at the McDowell Creek Park exit, and follow signs for 10 paved miles. To drive here from the east, turn north off Highway 20 at the west end of Sweet Home and follow signs 8.5 miles to the park.

The county park has three parking areas accessing the falls. Stop at the first lot, marked "Royal Terrace Falls," to hike through the park on the recommended 1.7-mile loop. Cross the creek on a large footbridge and follow the main trail left through a lush, low-elevation forest of mossy bigleaf maple, alder, and Douglas fir. Look for large white trilliums and sourgrass blooming in March. Sword fern, snowberry, and Oregon grape add to the greenery.

After 0.2 mile come to a long footbridge at the base of lacy Royal Terrace Falls, a 119-foot triple-decker. Cross the footbridge and continue, avoiding side trails to the left. At the far end of yet another footbridge, turn right. The trail next crosses the road and continues 0.2 mile to Crystal Pool, with its 20-foot cascade. Beyond this fall the trail crosses the creek and climbs 2 flights of stairs to a massive wooden viewpoint structure perched on the lip of 39-foot Majestic Falls.

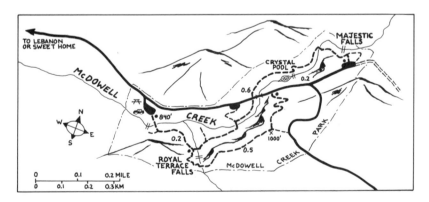

Majestic Falls.   Opposite: Fern fiddlehead.

From here, climb stone steps to the upper parking lot.

To complete the hiking loop, walk down the paved road 0.2 mile. Just before the highway crosses the creek, turn left onto an unmarked trail. This path switchbacks up to the canyon rim, with views across the valley through tall firs. Keep right for 0.4 mile to a fenced viewpoint at the top of Royal Terrace Falls. From here steep, dilapidated stone stairs lead down to the familiar loop trail; turn left 0.2 mile to the car.

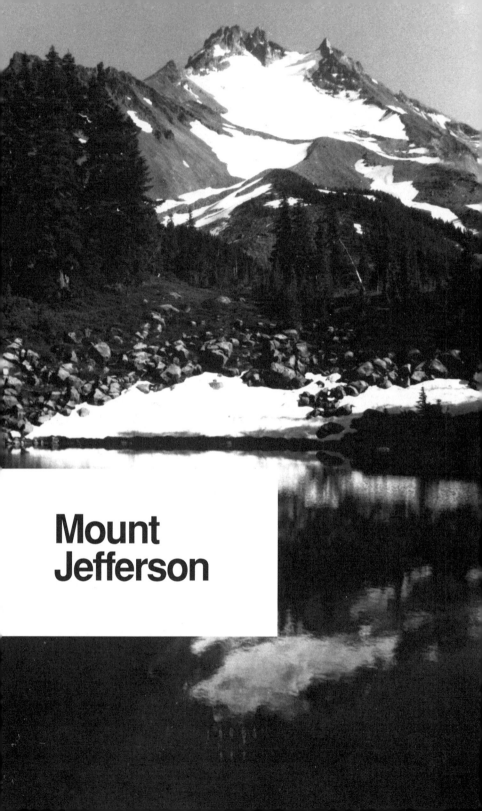

Mount
Jefferson

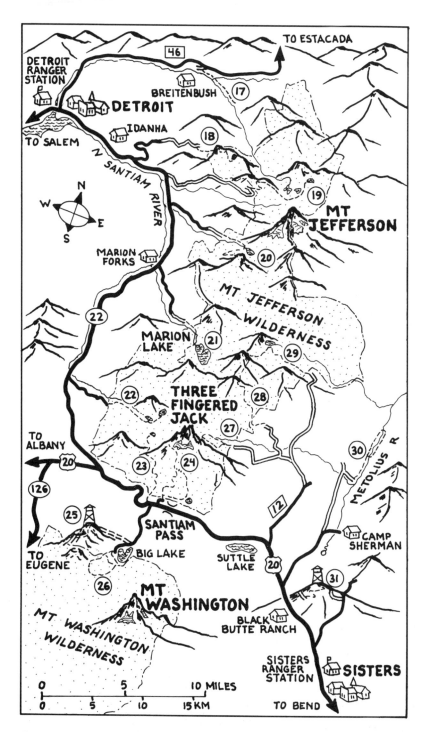

Opposite: Unnamed lake at Jefferson Park (Hike #19).

17   South Breitenbush Gorge

Easy
3.7 miles one-way with shuttle, or
6.4 miles round-trip to Roaring Creek
700 feet elevation gain
Open except in winter storms
Map: Breitenbush Hot Springs (USGS)

An easy walk through an old-growth forest, this hike follows the South Breitenbush River to a rocky narrows where the river churns through a 100-yard-long slot. If you shuttle a second car to the upper trailhead you can walk the path one-way. But you won't regret walking both directions along this pleasant forest trail.

Start at the Breitenbush Guard Station. To get there, turn off Highway 22 in Detroit at the sign for Breitenbush River, drive 11 miles on paved Road 46 (1.5 miles past the Breitenbush Campground), and turn sharply right onto gravel Road 050 to the rustic guard station — marked only by an "Information" sign on the door. Park here and walk 130 yards further on Road 050 to the trailhead on the left.

The trail promptly reaches the North Fork Breitenbush River, a raging, 50-foot-wide stream with broad gravel bars flanked by alder and tall red cedars. The old footbridge washed out in a 1990 flood; the trail now detours briefly downstream to a new bridge — a large fallen log with handrails. Then the trail climbs away from the river through a forest carpeted with delicate, shiny-leaved twinflowers. Rhododendrons bloom here in June.

The path next joins the South Fork Breitenbush but follows at a respectful distance, so river views are infrequent. At the 2-mile mark enter an area hard hit

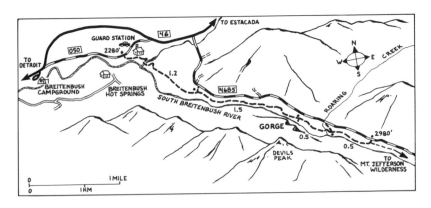

Footbridge at Roaring Creek.   Opposite: Ruffed grouse.

by a 1990 winter windstorm. In places two-thirds of the large trees fell, closing the trail for over a year.

At a small sign on the right announcing the South Breitenbush Gorge, take a short side trail down to this water-sculpted, 40-foot-deep rock chasm. This makes a nice lunch spot, but don't turn back to the car yet. The trail's next half mile is the prettiest of all, with river views and a scenic footbridge over mossy Roaring Creek.

If you've left a shuttle car ahead, continue 0.5 mile to the upper trailhead, taking the *second* left turn after Roaring Creek. To drive to this trailhead from paved Road 46, turn south for 2.6 miles on gravel Road 4685 (0.5 miles east of the guard station's turnoff), ignoring the first two trailheads. Park at the third trailhead, a poorly marked pullout on the right, half a mile past Roaring Creek.

Other Hiking Options

Like a longer hike? The trail continues 3 miles upriver, ending at Road 4685 a few hundred yards before the well-marked South Breitenbush Trailhead to Jefferson Park and Bear Point. Though scenic, this 3-mile section is unsigned and a little rough; it is the original tread used by staff of the former Bear Point lookout tower.

18 Triangulation Peak

Easy
4.2 miles round-trip
700 feet elevation gain
Open July through October
Map: Mt. Bruno (USGS)

The monumental view of Mt. Jefferson is reason enough to climb to Triangulation Peak's former lookout site. But there's a bonus if you're willing to scramble cross-country a few hundred yards: Boca Cave, a hidden, 60-foot-high cavern gaping from the peak's flank.

Start by driving Highway 22 east of Idanha 1 mile. Turn north onto McCoy Creek Road 2233 for 9.2 miles (1.3 miles past the road's right-hand turn at a winter sports building), and park on the right at spur Road 635. The trailhead sign is 100 feet down this spur, on the right.

The hike's first 1.5 miles are a nearly level stroll through a mountain hemlock forest, with big, white trilliums blooming once the snow is gone in late June. At the half-mile mark, pass a large clearcut on the left with a bumper crop of sun-loving huckleberries and a view of Mt. Hood.

The final 0.6 mile is much steeper. Turn right at a trail junction and switchback up past the base of Spire Rock's impressive monolith. Until mid-July expect to cross a few patches of snow on the trail. Finally the path reaches an open saddle and curves to the right, toward the site of the former lookout tower atop a rocky knob. Mt. Jefferson looms to the east, just 7 miles away. Snowpeaks from Diamond Peak to Mt. Rainier mark the horizon.

Boca Cave is hidden a few hundred yards from the summit, but only experienced hikers should attempt to find it, for there is no path and parts of the

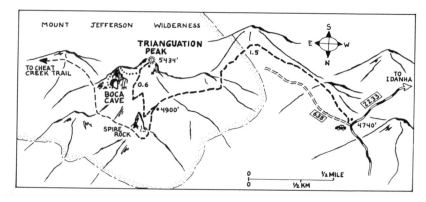

route are treacherously steep. To find it, hike back down the trail 200 yards to a saddle, turn right, and walk cross-country to Triangulation Peak's second, lower summit hump. Then continue another 200 yards toward Mt. Jefferson on a scramble trail that descends to the right around a rock outcropping, reaching a cliff edge. The cave is hidden at the bottom of this cliff. Get there by scrambling around the cliff to the right, down a steep, forested slope. The dome-shaped, 100-foot-deep cavern has a sloping floor of red cinders and a well-framed view of Mt. Jefferson. Digging or otherwise disturbing the cave is prohibited by law.

Other Hiking Options

With a car shuttle, you can descend from Triangulation Peak via the pleasant Cheat Creek Trail, upping the day's mileage to 8.2. Hike down to the trail junction by Spire Rock and turn right. This path contours around the peak to a scenic ridgecrest with fields of wildflowers and views up to Boca Cave (inaccessible from this side). After 2.6 miles, fork right onto the Cheat Creek Trail, which descends steeply through Wild Cheat Meadow and along rushing Cheat Creek, losing 1700 feet of elevation. To drive to the Cheat Creek Trailhead, follow Highway 22 east of Idanha 5.6 miles and turn left on Whitewater Road 2243 for 3.3 miles to the "Cheat Creek" sign.

Boca Cave and Mt. Jefferson.   Opposite: Marsh marigolds.

19   Jefferson Park

Moderate
10.2 miles round-trip
1800 feet elevation gain
Open mid-July to mid-October
Map: Mt. Jefferson Wilderness (USFS)

Oregon's second tallest mountain rises like a wall from the lake-dotted wildflower meadows of Jefferson Park. The view of Mt. Jefferson is so impressive and the meadows are so delightful to explore that the area shows signs of overuse.

On August weekends as many as 500 people roam this corner of the Wilderness. Many of the lakeshores, once green with vegetation, are roped off for restoration. Wilderness rangers strictly enforce restrictions: campfires are banned throughout the area and camping within 250 feet of the lakes is only permitted at approved sites marked with an imbedded post.

To visit this alpine treasure without damaging it or fighting crowds, *do not* come on August weekends. Wait for the clear, crisp weather of September — or come in late July, when the wildflowers (and, alas, the mosquitoes) are at their peak. Or, visit only as a day trip. If you insist on backpacking, bring a stove, a permit, and the energy to seek out one of the remote, forested corners of the park for your camp.

To find the trailhead, drive Highway 22 east from Detroit 10.3 miles (or 21 miles north of the Santiam Y junction) to Whitewater Road 2243. Follow this gravel route 7.4 miles to its end at the parking area in a clearcut.

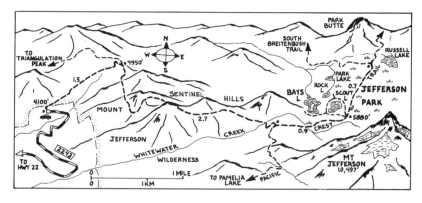

Bays Lake and Park Butte. *Opposite: Shooting stars.*

The trail starts out by switchbacking into an old-growth Douglas fir forest with a lush mat of twinflower and prince's pine. The well-graded path climbs steadily, entering a higher-elevation forest of true firs and beargrass. After 1.5 miles, reach a trail junction at the ridgecrest and turn right.

The path climbs east along the ridge for another mile, crosses a saddle, and then levels out. Breathtaking views of Mt. Jefferson begin here. At the 3.9-mile mark, a footbridge crosses Whitewater Creek in a meadow with shooting star, larkspur, and bleeding heart.

At the Pacific Crest Trail junction, turn left. For the next 0.9 mile the trailside meadows become larger and prettier until the path reaches Jefferson Park — a vast plateau of heather, Indian paintbrush, lupine, and clumps of windblown mountain hemlock. Here, unfortunately, a confusion of trails proliferate — left to Bays Lake, right to the head of Whitewater Creek. To follow the PCT, keep straight to the first glimpse of Scout Lake, then veer right.

One way to explore the area is to follow the PCT 0.8 mile across the park to large Russell Lake and return cross-country, either south through the heather or southwest to find the hidden lakes. Plan on a swim, for the lakes here are among Oregon's most inviting.

20 Pamelia Lake

Easy (to Pamelia Lake)
4.4 miles round-trip
800 feet elevation gain
Open May through November
Map: Mt. Jefferson Wilderness (USFS)

Difficult (to Grizzly Peak)
10 miles round-trip
2700 feet elevation gain
Open July through October

The popular trail to Pamelia Lake has something for everyone: an easy creekside forest stroll for the novice hiker, a lake with a mountain reflection for the meditative, and an optional, strenuous viewpoint climb for the go-getters. What's the catch? Only that the trail *is* so popular.

To limit crowds, the Forest Service is requiring that hikers and campers headed for Pamelia Lake in the summer of 1996 pick up a permit in advance at the Detroit Ranger Station. Permits will only be issued to 20 groups a day. Camping at the lake is only allowed at approved sites marked by a post. After 1996, call the Detroit Ranger Station at (503) 854-3366 for the latest rules.

Drive to the trailhead by taking Highway 22 to Pamelia Road 2246 (the turnoff is between mileposts 62 and 63). Follow Road 2246 for 3.7 miles to the trailhead parking lot at its end.

The wide trail begins in an enchanting forest so thickly carpeted with moss that rocks and fallen logs soon become mere lumps in the green cushion. Trilliums and rhododendrons bloom profusely along the way in May and June. Vine maple and huckleberry turn scarlet in fall. In all seasons, noisy Pamelia Creek accompanies the trail with little whitewater scenes.

At the first glimpse of the lake, you come to a trail junction indicating Grizzly Peak to the right and the Pacific Crest Trail to the left. For the time being, ignore both and go straight ahead to inspect the lakeshore. The lake was formed when a rockslide pinched off a narrow glacial valley. Since the lake's outlet relies largely on subterranean seepage through the rocks, the water level varies seasonally. By summer, expect a reservoir-like beach. Walk to the right around the lakeshore for a noble view of Mt. Jefferson.

For a first-rate viewpoint, return to the trail junction and follow the sign to Grizzly Peak. This path crosses the lake's usually dry outlet and heads steadily up the peak's flank on a long traverse. The route is so well-graded the massive elevation gain seems less difficult than might be expected. After 1 mile the path switchbacks up to a tilted plateau where beargrass blooms put on a spectacular display approximately every third summer. After climbing 2.1 miles from the lake, the trail switchbacks at a cliff edge with the climb's first viewpoint.

Now here's a secret: this first viewpoint is in many ways a better goal than the actual summit of Grizzly Peak, a difficult 0.7-mile climb beyond. The bird's-eye view of Mt. Jefferson is identical from here, and this cliff edge offers a far better

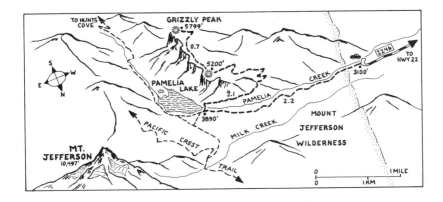

look down at Pamelia Lake. What's more, the path is snow-free to this point by mid-June, when drifts still clog the route ahead. On the other hand, only the actual summit has a view south across the Wilderness to the Three Sisters.

Other Hiking Options

The 1.1-mile hike north up to the Pacific Crest Trail's crossing of Milk Creek makes a nice side trip. Named for the silt-laden runoff of glaciers, Milk Creek pours down a rough-and-tumble canyon with a gaping view up Mt. Jefferson's slopes.

For a scenic backpacking trip, continue south 4 miles past Pamelia Lake to Hunts Cove. To make a 16-mile loop, return via the PCT.

Pamelia Lake and Mt. Jefferson.   Opposite: Lichen along the trail.

21 Marion Lake

Easy (to Marion Lake)
6 miles round-trip
800 feet elevation gain
Open mid-May to mid-November
Map: Mt. Jefferson Wilderness (USFS)

Difficult (to Marion Mountain)
11.2 miles round-trip
2000 feet elevation gain
Open mid-June through October

Generations of Oregon families have hiked to Marion Lake to escape the Willamette Valley's summer heat. Traditions die hard. For many people, this mile-long lake remains the only familiar destination in the Mt. Jefferson Wilderness — even though much of the lakeshore is roped off for restoration, the fishing is hampered by algae, and the trail is trampled to an 8-foot-wide promenade. Backpackers are required to bring permits.

But if you avoid the crowds by coming any time *other* than summer weekends, the easy walk to Marion Lake does have attractions, notably Marion Falls and a rock peninsula with a distant view of Three Fingered Jack. A long, optional side trip up to Marion Mountain's former lookout site provides a bit more exercise, as well as a frontal view of the elusive Mt. Jefferson.

To reach the trailhead, drive Highway 22 to Marion Forks (near milepost 67). Turn east onto Marion Creek Road 2255 and drive 5.4 miles to the parking lot at road's end.

The trail begins with a nearly level half-mile stretch through deep woods. Then the route climbs 1.3 miles to the outlet of forest-rimmed Lake Ann. Listen for the gurgle of water beneath the trail's rocky tread; the outlet is wholly subterranean. This portion of Lake Ann's shoreline is recovering from overuse; camping is banned.

Beyond Lake Ann 0.4 mile bear right at a trail junction, following the Marion Lake Outlet Trail. Up this route 200 yards, watch for an unmarked side trail to the right. Follow this path 0.2 mile down to Marion Falls, an impressive but seldom visited cascade. Then return to the main trail and continue half a mile to a junction at the footbridge across the lake's outlet. Both fishing and camping are prohibited near the outlet. It's also illegal to enter any of the restoration areas cordoned off by twine and signs; seedlings have been planted to help vegetation return.

If you're just taking the easy loop trip, turn left at the outlet, following the shoreline trail 0.4 mile to a rock peninsula. This stretch of shore, and the peninsula itself, are reserved strictly for day use. On the peninsula's north side, look for smoothed, exposed bedrock — evidence this area was scoured by Ice Age glaciers. At a trail junction just beyond the peninsula, turn left to return to the car.

Marion Lake.   Opposite: Sign on overused lakeshore area.

Don't try walking entirely around the lake, since swamps at the far end are impassable. Instead, if you're interested in a longer hike, why not climb to Marion Mountain's former lookout site for a look around? Return to the footbridge at the lake outlet and take the Blue Lake Trail, climbing steadily on a long traverse for 1 mile. The forest changes here to a drier mix of lodgepole pine, huckleberry, and bear grass. At a junction by a pond, turn right onto the less-steep Pine Ridge Trail for 0.8 mile to another junction. Watch for a fork in the trail; turn left at a small sign for Marion Mountain and ascend 0.8 mile to a rocky ridgecrest with a view of Three-Fingered Jack. Go left along the ridgecrest 100 yards to the lookout site and a sweeping view across Marion Lake's valley to Mt. Jefferson.

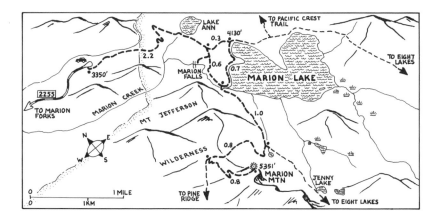

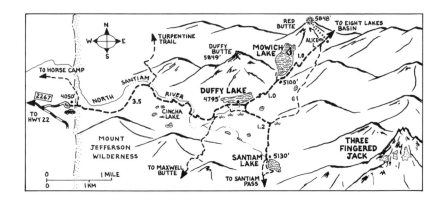

22   Duffy Lake

Moderate (to Duffy Lake)
7 miles round-trip
800 feet elevation gain
Open early June to early November
Map: Mt. Jefferson Wilderness (USFS)

Difficult (to Red Butte)
12 miles round-trip
1800 feet elevation gain
Open July through October

The forests west of Three Fingered Jack conceal dozens of lakes, meadows, and buttes. Of these, Duffy Lake is the easiest and most frequently visited goal, offering a tranquil reflection of craggy Duffy Butte. For a more challenging destination, continue past Mowich Lake to Red Butte, a cinder cone with a map-like view of the entire area.

Drive to the trailhead by taking Highway 22 to Big Meadows Road 2267 (the turnoff is 5.7 miles north of the Santiam Y junction, or 25 miles from Detroit). Follow Road 2267 east 3 miles to its end at a turnaround.

The wide, well-graded Duffy Trail climbs gradually for 1.5 miles through a stately forest of old Douglas fir and hemlock. Then, after the Turpentine Trail splits off to the left, the route levels along the North Santiam River for another 1.1 miles to a bridgeless river crossing.

This crossing is no problem in August or September when the river is dry. In early summer and late fall, however, the stream can flow 20 feet wide. There are stepping stones, but it's safer to bring old tennis shoes and wade.

Beyond the crossing 0.4 mile ignore a trail to the Maxwell Trailhead splitting off to the right. The main path follows beside the meandering river's meadows to a 4-way trail junction; go straight and come to a footbridge across the (often dry) outlet of Duffy Lake.

Backpackers must bring permits and cannot use campfires within 100 feet of the lake or the trail. Several severely overused sites have been closed for wilderness restoration.

If you're headed onward and upward to Red Butte, continue along the lake, taking the route signed to Eight Lakes. A 1-mile walk leads to a delightful sandy beach at Mowich Lake, a steep-shored lake with a large forested island. Next the trail climbs 1 mile to a junction. Continue straight on the Blue Lake Trail a few hundred yards to little Alice Lake in a meadow on the left. From here Red Butte is obvious, and so is the cross-country route up this steep cinder cone to a delightful view of the Eight Lakes Basin, Mt. Jefferson, Three Fingered Jack, and the Three Sisters.

Other Hiking Options

Santiam Lake, with its wildflower meadows and its reflection of Three Fingered Jack, makes another worthwhile destination. To get there, hike 0.2 mile past Duffy Lake's outlet and turn right for 1 mile following signs for Santiam Pass. This route connects with Hike #23, making a 9.8-mile, one-way hike possible for those with a car shuttle.

Duffy Lake and Duffy Butte.   Opposite: Bunchberry.

23   Berley Lakes

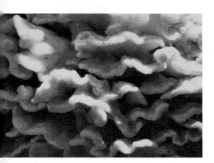

Easy (to Lower Berley Lake)
6.8 miles round-trip
500 feet elevation gain
Open July through October
Map: Mt. Jefferson Wilderness (USFS)

Moderate (to Santiam Lake)
10.2 miles round-trip
800 feet elevation gain

The Pacific Crest Trail is designed to bypass most of the fragile high country lakes, but an earlier route along the Cascade crest, the old Skyline Trail, intentionally dipped from lake to lake. This hike follows a heavily used portion of that older crest trail from Santiam Pass to the lakes and cinder-strewn meadows at the base of Three Fingered Jack.

Although you can start this hike at the well-marked Pacific Crest Trail parking lot, it's no further and much less crowded to start at the Skyline Trail's original trailhead. To find it, drive Highway 20 to Santiam Pass. Opposite the turnoff for the Hoodoo Ski Area — and 100 yards west — turn north onto an unmarked road leading 50 yards to a parking lot and a sign for the Santiam Lodge Trail.

The nearly level trail traverses a subalpine forest well-stocked with huckleberries, beargrass, bracken fern, and queen's cup. On this entire hike the path is wide and dusty from long use. The soil itself is dusty with volcanic ash from geologically recent eruptions of Maxwell Butte and Red Butte.

After 1.7 miles turn left, following the sign for the Eight Lakes Basin. Half a mile beyond this junction and just before a small meadow, pass the almost unrecognizable, charred remains of Jack Shelter, once one of a string of historic shelters along the former Skyline Trail.

Berley Lakes are not visible from the trail, nor is the side trail to them marked, so watch closely for the turnoff. After hiking 3.2 miles from the trailhead, crest

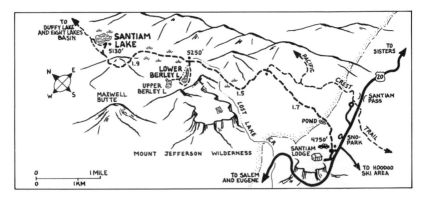

Three Fingered Jack from Lower Berley Lake.   Opposite: Chicken of the woods (fungus).

a rise and come to a small campsite. Here, just before the main trail crosses a small, rocky creekbed (usually dry), turn left and follow a side trail along the creekbed 100 yards to Lower Berley Lake. Continue on the somewhat rough path to the lake's far end, with a nice beach, a small meadow, and a view of Three Fingered Jack. A bit further around the lake an even fainter route heads up to Upper Berley Lake, a few hundred yards northwest.

To get to Santiam Lake, return to the main trail and continue left. This path crosses a broad sandy plain, climbs over a low forested ridge, and finally forks. The main route, to the left, bypasses Santiam Lake. The right fork goes along the lakeshore, featuring top-to-bottom views of Three Fingered Jack. The lake itself is scenically set in a broad basin with scattered meadows and subalpine fir.

At both Santiam Lake and the Berley Lakes, backpackers must bring permits and cannot use campfires within 100 feet of the fragile lakeshores. Tent in sandy openings (not on meadow vegetation!) hidden away from the shore.

Other Hiking Options

This trail connects with the route to Santiam Lake described in Hike #22. With a car shuttle, the combined one-way trip is 9.8 miles.

24   Three Fingered Jack

Moderate (to viewpoint)
10.4 miles round-trip
1400 feet elevation gain
Open late July to mid-October
Map: Mt. Jefferson Wilderness (USFS)

Difficult (return via Martin Lake)
11.7-mile loop
1600 feet elevation gain

This demanding portion of the Pacific Crest Trail climbs from Santiam Pass to a viewpoint on the timberline slopes beneath Three Fingered Jack's summit crags. Experienced hikers comfortable with a short cross-country scramble can return on a slightly longer loop trail past Martin, Booth, and Square Lakes. Backpackers must bring permits.

Begin at the Pacific Crest Trail parking area 0.2 mile down a paved entrance road from Highway 20 at Santiam Pass. The forest here is a high-elevation mix of lodgepole pine and true fir, dotted with beargrass. Down the trail 100 yards, turn left onto the actual PCT. At the Square Lake Trail junction 0.2 mile beyond, go straight. After another 1.2 mile, reach a junction at the base of a rocky knoll. Keep right on the PCT, which now heads more steeply up the side of a forested ridge.

At the 3.5-mile mark the trail finally gains the ridgetop and the first impressive views: east to Black Butte, south to the Three Sisters, west to Maxwell Butte, and ahead to the tip of Three Fingered Jack. After a stretch along the ridgecrest, the path traverses to the right across a steep, rocky slope high above blue-green Martin Lake. Then come 3 switchbacks and a traverse to the left through steep alpine country. Finally the trail rounds a bend for a first view of Three Fingered Jack's west face. But don't stop yet. In another 0.2 mile the path turns a sharper corner to an even more spectacular view.

The peak's crags are actually the eroded core of a much larger, smooth-sided volcano. The red and black stripes are remnants of the lava layers that built up the original cone. Note the ascent trail scarring the scree high on the mountain's shoulder; you can often spot climbers on the jagged skyline above.

Of course the easiest route back is on the PCT. But experienced hikers with some extra energy can try a loop past 3 lakes instead. Hike back down the PCT 1.5 miles to the ridgecrest overlooking Martin Lake to the east. There's no trail down to Martin Lake, and the route is very steep. Start at a low spot in the ridge where the slope is the least rocky, take a good look at the lake below, and head directly downhill through the open woods. The bearing for this 0.3-mile cross-country descent is due east, but simply aiming downhill will hit the lake, since it fills the only outlet to this narrow valley.

At Martin Lake, walk around the shore to a charming meadow at the lake's far end. From here a clear trail (not shown on any topographic map) descends

Three Fingered Jack from the Pacific Crest Trail.   Opposite: Booth Lake.

half a mile to the large and unmistakable Booth Lake Trail. There is no trail junction sign here, and in fact a downed tree disguises this end of the Martin Lake path, making it virtually unfindable for anyone hiking the opposite direction — so do not attempt this loop in reverse.

Turn right on the Booth Lake Trail for 1.7 miles to a junction at large, heavily used Square Lake. Then turn right on the Square Lake Trail for 2.2 less interesting miles to the PCT and the return route to the car.

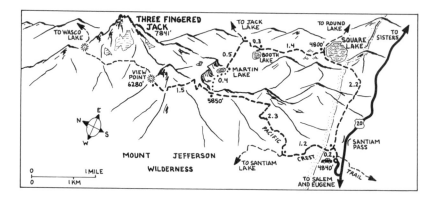

25   Sand Mountain Lookout

Easy
1.3-mile loop
400 feet elevation gain
Open July through October
Map: Clear Lake (USGS)

In the 1940s Oregon boasted more than 800 fire lookout towers, staffed each summer by isolation-tolerant souls willing to trade civilization's comforts for a glass-walled viewpoint in the wilderness. Now that most fire-spotting work is done by airplane, only about 100 towers remain, and only a fraction are staffed.

Nostalgia for the old towers runs particularly high among the *children* of the original staffers. Don Allen, for one, grew up spending summers on this cratered cinder cone near Santiam Pass. Years after the original tower burned in 1968, he founded the Sand Mountain Society to protect the area from off-road vehicle damage and to rebuild a tower with painstaking historical accuracy. Volunteers — many with lookout experience on other summits — joined in the effort. They salvaged a 1930s-style tower originally from Whisky Peak in the Rogue River National Forest. They rebuilt authentic furniture based on early photographs. They installed a functioning, antique fire-sighting table for locating smoke plumes.

Now these volunteers staff the finished tower each summer, welcoming visitors. And they actually do spot quite a few otherwise unreported wildfires, for this little cinder cone offers one of the most comprehensive panoramas in the entire Central Oregon Cascades.

To drive to Sand Mountain, take Highway 20 to Santiam Pass, turn south at the Hoodoo Ski Area sign, and follow the paved Big Lake Road 3.1 miles to a

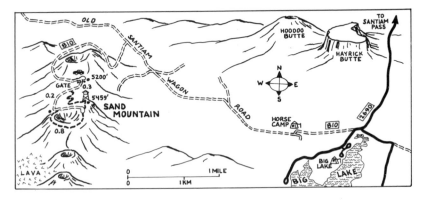

major fork. Keep right toward Big Lake Campground, but after another 200 yards turn right again onto dirt Road 810. This is a remnant of the Old Santiam Wagon Road, a toll route built from Albany to Central Oregon between 1861 and 1868.

The historic track remains unimproved, and may be impassable in wet weather. Drive passenger cars with caution to avoid large rocks and ruts. Follow Road 810 as it jogs to the left at a primitive horse camp 0.9 mile from the Big Lake Road. At the 1.5-mile mark, go straight at a fork. After 2.4 miles, go straight at a 4-way junction. Finally, 2.9 miles from the paved road, turn left toward the lookout and climb 1.5 miles to a parking area at a locked gate.

Hike up the closed road 200 yards and turn left on a trail switchbacking up to the tower. Mt. Washington is particularly impressive from here, rising above Big Lake. To the west, lava flows snake from their source at Sand Mountain to Clear Lake — which formed when these flows dammed the McKenzie River 3000 years ago. In the Old Cascades beyond, look for Iron Mountain's distinctive thumb and the Three Pyramids' peaks.

After soaking up the view, hike on to the closed road's upper terminus and continue on a path around the crater rim. Watch for well-camouflaged, thumb-sized horned toads scampering among the cinders. Return to the car via the road.

Sand Mountain Lookout.   Opposite: Horned toad.

26   Patjens Lakes

Easy
6-mile loop
400 feet elevation gain
Open late June through October
Map: Mt. Washington Wilderness
     (USFS)

Hidden in the high lodgepole pine forests south of Santiam Pass, these small lakes reflect rugged, spire-topped Mt. Washington. The easy loop trail here also passes a remote beach of Big Lake, where you can wash off the trail dust with a refreshing swim. Mosquitoes are a problem the first half of July. If you're backpacking, bring a permit.

To find the trailhead, drive Highway 20 to Santiam Pass, turn south at the Hoodoo Ski Area sign, and follow the paved Big Lake Road 4 miles (0.7 mile past the Big Lake Campground entrance) to a hiker-symbol sign at the trailhead on the right.

After just 0.1 mile the trail forks, with signs pointing to the Patjens Lakes in both directions — since the loop's hikable either way. Take the right-hand fork and gradually descend through a dry forest where bear grass and lupine provide occasional July blooms. After 1 mile the trail follows the long meadow of a (dry) snowmelt creek. Then the path gradually climbs to a low pass, offering glimpses north to Sand Mountain's double hump of red cinders (with the lookout tower described in Hike #25).

On the far side of the ridge the trail descends through several small bracken meadows brightened with stalks of scarlet gilia. Above the trees look for (left to

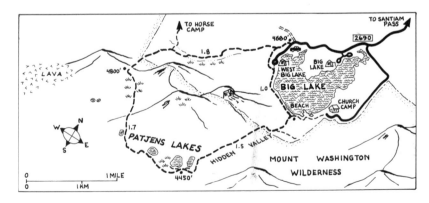

Early summer morning at the Patjens Lakes. *Opposite: Lupine leaves.*

right) Mt. Washington, Belknap Crater's black shield, the Three Sisters, the Husband, and Scott Mountain's long, low rise.

The first Patjen Lake is a pond on the right. Half a mile beyond is a more substantial lake on the left, with a mostly brushy shore. The third lake is the largest and most attractive, surrounded by meadows. The last lake's water level varies seasonally, leaving a wide, muddy beach.

After exploring the lakes continue 1.5 miles to an unmarked trail junction. Go left and promptly come to a sandy beach with a view across Big Lake to cliff-rimmed Hayrick Butte. By late summer the water's warm enough for excellent swimming here. The trail continues 0.6 mile around the lakeshore to another unmarked fork. Either go left to return to the car via the loop trail, or go right to the West Big Lake Campground and a short walk along the road to the car.

Three Fingered Jack from the lower meadow.   Below: Columbine.

27   Canyon Creek Meadows

Easy (to lower meadow)
4.3-mile loop
400 feet elevation gain
Open mid-July through October
Map: Mt. Jefferson Wilderness (USFS)

Moderate (to viewpoint)
7.3-mile loop
1400 feet elevation gain
Open August through October

One of the easiest routes to the High Cascades' wildflower meadows, this short loop is ideal for children and amblers. More energetic hikers can continue up a steep glacial moraine to an ice-filled cirque lake and a breathtaking viewpoint beneath Three Fingered Jack's summit pinnacles. For solitude, however, skip summer weekends when this trail attracts 60 to 100 visitors a day.

Turn off Highway 20 at the "Wilderness Trailheads" sign 8 miles east of Santiam Pass (1 mile east of Suttle Lake). Drive north 3.7 miles on paved Road

12, continue straight on gravel Road 1230 for 1.5 miles, and then turn left onto Road 1234, climbing 5 miles to the trailhead at the primitive Jack Lake campground.

Start hiking on the trail to the right, which skirts Jack Lake's shore and climbs to the Wilderness boundary and a well-marked fork at the 0.3-mile point: the start of the loop.

To limit the number of people you meet, the Forest Service asks that you hike the loop clockwise. So bear left at this junction, climb gradually through the lodgepole pines, pass 2 ponds atop a small ridge, and descend to the lower meadow. Here the view of Three Fingered Jack's snow-clad crags emerges and the wildflower displays begin in earnest. Peak season for the masses of blue lupine and red Indian paintbrush is the end of July — a trade-off, because mosquitoes are still a nuisance and snowdrifts usually still block the trail to the upper meadow until August. At any season, do not trample these delicate alpine gardens. Stay on the main trail and choose a picnic spot amid trees. Backpackers should bring permits and should camp at least 100 feet from trails or water (please, *not* atop fragile meadow vegetation).

If you still have plenty of energy, continue 0.7 mile up the trail to the rim of the rock-strewn upper meadow — actually a glacial outwash plain. From here the 0.8-mile route to the 6500-foot-elevation viewpoint becomes less distinct. Climb south up a steep, rocky moraine to a notch overlooking a stunning, green cirque lake at the foot of Three Fingered Jack's glacier. Next the path follows the somewhat precarious crest of the moraine, scrambling steeply up to the windy saddle, where the view stretches from Mt. Jefferson to the Three Sisters. Sharp eyes can often spot climbers on the spires of Three Fingered Jack.

To return via the loop, hike back to the bottom of the lower meadow and turn left. This path follows Canyon Creek past a fascinating beaver workshop, where dozens of large pines have been ringed and felled. Rings 6 feet above the ground prove the beavers are active when winter snowdrifts remain.

Half a mile beyond the beaver trees join the trail from Wasco Lake — but before turning right to return to the car, follow the sound of falling water to a footbridge below the first of Canyon Creek Falls' 2 lovely, 12-foot cascades.

Other Hiking Options

For an easy side trip, leave the loop hike at Canyon Creek Falls and walk a nearly level 0.7 mile to deep, clear blue Wasco Lake.

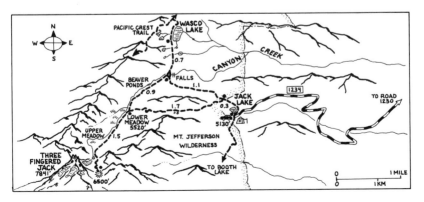

28 Rockpile Lake

Difficult (to Rockpile Lake)
10.4 miles round-trip
2100 feet elevation gain
Open August through October
Map: Marion Lake (USGS)

Difficult (to South Cinder Peak)
13.6 miles round-trip
2600 feet elevation gain

Even when crowds throng other parts of the Mt. Jefferson Wilderness you'll probably find solitude on a little-known trail recently built up Bear Valley. This view-packed route climbs a ridge to Rockpile Lake, a small jewel set right on the Cascade crest. For an even better view continue an optional 1.6 miles along the crest to South Cinder Peak, a volcanic cone overlooking most of the Central Oregon Cascades.

To find the Bear Valley Trailhead, turn off Highway 20 at the "Wilderness Trailheads" sign 8 miles east of Santiam Pass (or 12 miles west of Sisters). Drive north 3.7 miles on paved Road 12, continue straight on gravel Road 1230 for 1.5 miles, veer left onto Road 1234 for 0.8 mile, and turn right onto Road 1235 for 3.9 miles to a turnaround at its end.

After 100 feet the trail forks. Don't continue straight on the route to Minto Lake; instead, switchback to the right on a path that descends for a while before climbing a sunny, open ridge. Views emerge of Three Fingered Jack, Black Butte, and then Mt. Jefferson. Trailside bushes on this dry slope include pungent snowbrush (*Ceanothus*), tough-limbed manzanita, and chinkapin. The trail itself was cleared of this brush by a Redmond fire-fighting crew to keep in shape for building fire lines.

After 2 miles, cross the Wilderness boundary and then turn left on the Two Springs Trail. This path climbs steadily for 3.1 miles through a forest of lichen-

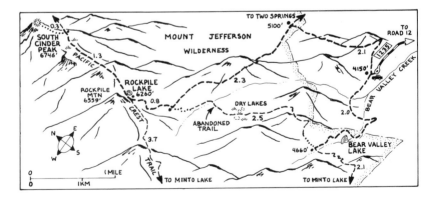

draped mountain hemlock. The trees give way to alpine meadows of heather and huckleberry just before the Pacific Crest Trail junction at Rockpile Lake. Camping in the lake's little, steep-sided basin is limited to sites marked by a post, and these sites are often occupied by PCT travelers. Permits are required.

Rockpile Lake offers a glimpse of the Three Sisters, but if you'd like a better view, continue 1.3 miles north along the scenic PCT. When the trail finally draws alongside of South Cinder Peak's red cone, leave the PCT and strike out cross-country to the left, cross an open cinder field, and slog up the very steep scramble trail to the summit. Mt. Jefferson looms to the north, conical Black Butte guards the Metolius Valley to the east, and on the western horizon, beyond Marion Lake, look for the Three Pyramids and square-topped Coffin Mountain.

Other Hiking Options

It's only 2.6 miles farther to return from Rockpile Lake on a scenic loop to the south. From Rockpile Lake, hike south 3.1 miles along a high portion of the PCT. At a junction in a saddle, turn left for 0.6 mile to a fork in the trail. At this point, Minto Lake is just out of sight to your right. To complete the loop, turn left on the Minto Tie Trail and descend 4.1 miles to your car in Bear Valley.

A second, shorter route down from Rockpile Lake follows the abandoned Bear Valley Trail down the viewless valley bottom — but this path has not been maintained since the new ridgetop route was completed in 1991.

Rockpile Lake.   Opposite: Woodpecker holes.

29   Carl Lake

Moderate (to Carl Lake)
10 miles round-trip
1000 feet elevation gain
Open mid-July through October
Map: Mt. Jefferson Wilderness (USFS)

Difficult (to South Cinder Peak)
14.2 miles round-trip
2200 feet elevation gain

There's lots to do at this deep, rock-rimmed alpine lake: explore the interesting shoreline, admire wildflowers, gather huckleberries, or take a challenging side trip to a viewpoint atop South Cinder Peak.

To start, turn off Highway 20 at the "Wilderness Trailheads" sign 8 miles east of Santiam Pass (or 12 miles west of Sisters). Drive north 3.7 miles on paved Road 12 and then continue straight on gravel Road 1230 for 8.3 miles to its end, following signs for the Cabot Lake Trailhead.

The trail's first 2 miles climb very gradually through a mixed forest. Many of the Douglas firs have been killed by tiny spruce budworms burrowing within the needles. This is not as tragic as it sounds, for the extra sunshine has encouraged the huckleberry bushes to put out masses of delicious blue fruit each August.

At the 2-mile mark go briefly right on a short, unsigned side trail to inspect forest-rimmed Cabot Lake. Then return to the main path, which now heads uphill in earnest. After a dozen switchbacks the trail levels somewhat, passing a series of three scenic ponds. A final level stretch leads to large, blue-green Carl Lake.

The trail leads left around the south shore, past small heather meadows with purple aster and white partridge foot. Though there is no trail around the lake's

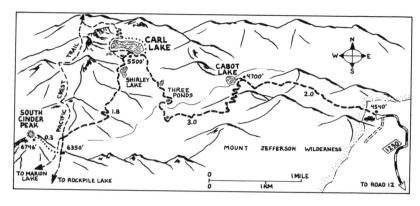

Carl Lake.   Opposite: Glacier-polished rock.

north shore, the mountain views are better there, and the bared bedrock rim is quite hikable. The north shore bears the marks of the Ice Age glacier which gouged out this lake's basin, polishing the bedrock smooth and sometimes grooving the surface as smaller rocks dragged beneath the heavy ice. Only a narrow rim now holds the lake back from the steep Cabot Creek Valley beyond. Atop this natural dam, bonsaied whitebark pines struggle in cracks. Clark's nutcrackers squawk, eyeing picnickers' sandwiches.

If you're backpacking, remember to bring a permit and to camp more than 100 feet from the shore or trail.

If you're interested in the challenging side trip up South Cinder Peak, take the turnoff for Shirley Lake in the middle of Carl Lake's south shore. This trail passes above Shirley Lake and traverses steadily up the sunny side of a steep, scenic valley. Expect huckleberries here, too. At an alpine pass, turn left on the Pacific Crest Trail for 0.2 mile until the red cone of South Cinder Peak is immediately to your right. Then strike off cross-country across a cinder flat and up the steep, loose slope. Views promptly unfold of Mt. Jefferson and the Three Sisters.

Other Hiking Options

By arranging a car shuttle to the Bear Valley Trailhead, you can connect the trip to South Cinder Peak with Hike #28 to Rockpile Lake, making for a 13.7-mile one-way hike. If you have no shuttle but lots of energy, follow the Pacific Crest Trail 2.1 miles north to a saddle and turn right on a different route to Carl Lake, making for a strenuous 16.4-mile loop.

Ponderosa pine along Metolius River Trail.   Opposite: Gushing springs.

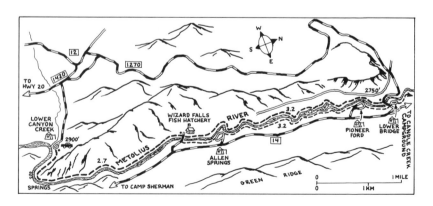

30   Metolius River

Easy (to Wizard Falls fish hatchery)
5.4 miles round-trip
100 feet elevation gain
Open all year
Maps: Candle Cr., Black Bu. (USGS)

The Metolius, most magical of all Oregon rivers, emerges fully grown at 50,000 gallons a minute from the arid base of Black Butte. Sample the river's wizardry with this easy hike along a section of the oasis-like riverbank. The trail passes sudden springs, reveals colorful bird life, and leads to a wonderfully visitable fish hatchery.

Turn north off Highway 20 near Black Butte at the sign to Camp Sherman. Drive straight on this paved road (#14), ignoring the right-hand fork labeled "Campgrounds." At the 5-mile mark, continue straight onto gravel Road 1420. After another 3 miles, turn right at a sign for Canyon Creek Campground and drive 1 mile to the West Metolius Trailhead, beside the river at the far end of the campground.

Just 0.3 mile down the trail, spectacular springs enter the river from the far bank, gushing like a dozen opened fire hydrants. The river winds through a steep canyon here with old-growth ponderosa pine and lots of May-June wildflowers: purple larkspur, yellow monkeyflower, and red columbine. A mile beyond the huge springs some smaller springs seep across the trail, muddying unwary hikers' tennis shoes.

At the 2-mile point the river's whitewater splits around a series of long islands, bushy with monkeyflower, lupine, and false hellebore. Birds delight in these islands. Look for broods of goslings paddling about, bright yellow tanagers hopping in streamside shrubs, and the peculiar robin-sized water ouzels that whir along the river's surface, at times diving to "fly" underwater.

Soon the trail reaches the rustic buildings and countless open-air concrete ponds of the Wizard Falls state fish hatchery. Wizard Falls itself, on a spring-fed side creek, dried up when its spring was tapped for the hatchery. Though there are no formal tours, friendly staff members always seem to be on hand to answer questions and show, for example, the indoor tank of two-headed fish. Fish food can be purchased from dispensing machines for 25 cents.

Other Hiking Options

Trails continue beyond the fish hatchery on both banks to the bridge at Lower Bridge Campground, making an additional 6.4-mile loop tempting. From the hatchery, continue 3.2 miles along the quiet west bank, cross the river, and return on the east bank through 2 campgrounds.

31 Black Butte Lookout

Moderate
3.8 miles round-trip
1600 feet elevation gain
Open July through October
Map: Black Butte (USGS)

Plunked in the midst of the Central Oregon plateau, Black Butte looks like a misplaced mountain. This symmetrical volcano formed before the last Ice Age along the same fault that uplifted Green Ridge's scarp to the north. The resulting 3000-foot pile of cinders is one of the tallest such cones in the state. The eruption buried the Metolius River, creating Black Butte Ranch's swampy meadows on one side of the mountain and Metolius Springs on the other, where the river now emerges.

The butte's unusual placement east of the High Cascades makes it ideal as a fire lookout site. In 1910 one of Oregon's earliest fire detection structures was built here: a simple platform wedged between two adjacent treetops. That original tower is gone, but later structures are intact: a cupola-style building from 1924, an 85-foot tower erected by the Civilian Conservation Corps in 1934, and a new, 65-foot tower built in 1995. In 1979 a one-room log cabin was constructed in Sisters, disassembled, and flown by helicopter to the butte's summit to provide the staff with more comfortable quarters.

A steep but view-packed trail climbs to Black Butte's summit. To find the trailhead, turn off Highway 22 on Green Ridge Road 11 (west of Sisters 5.5 miles, or 2.5 miles east of Black Butte Ranch). Follow paved Road 11 north for 3.8 miles.

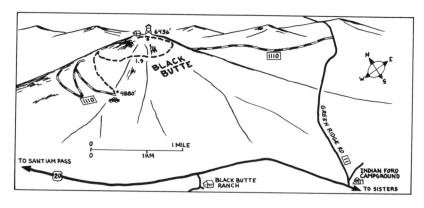

Cupola-style lookout atop Black Butte.   Opposite: Abandoned lookout tower.

Then turn left onto gravel Road 1110 for 5.1 miles to a parking area at the road's end.

The trail climbs steadily through a forest of orange-barked old-growth ponderosa pine. After 1.1 mile, the route crosses a treeless slope with manzanita bushes and a variety of wildflowers: yellow balsamroot, scarlet gilia, white yarrow, and blue lupine. The golf courses of Black Butte Ranch appear as miniature meadows in the forest far below.

Next the path climbs sharply — a hot, dusty stretch that makes this hike tough for small children. The trail gains the butte's broad, eastern ridge amidst wind-stunted whitebark pines and follows the ridge up to the top.

Do not attempt to climb or enter the lookout structures. The 85-foot tower was declared unsafe and closed in 1990. The log cabin is the lookout staff's residence; respect their privacy. And bring your own drinking water, as the staff has none to spare. They diligently collect snow each spring and allow it to melt, filling a concrete cistern.

Bend
Area

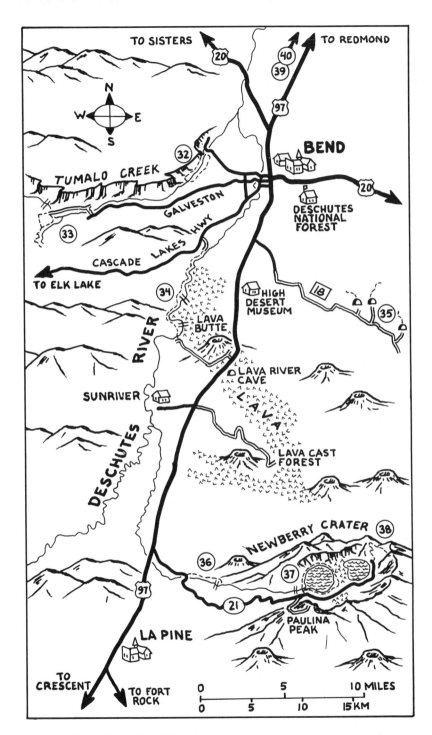

Opposite: Tumalo Falls (Hike #33).

32   Shevlin Park

Easy
5-mile loop
300 feet elevation gain
Open year-round
Map: Shevlin Park (USGS)

This canyon rim trail along Tumalo Creek begins just 4 miles from downtown Bend, yet feels surprisingly remote. Even the picnickers who gather in Shevlin Park's creekside meadows often overlook this unmarked path among the ponderosa pines. The hike is particularly welcome in winter or early spring, for it usually remains open when other Central Oregon trails are under snow. Expect some mountain bikers, for a roadside bicycle path connects the park with Bend.

To find the park, drive west on Greenwood Avenue from downtown Bend. Continue straight on what becomes Newport Avenue and then Shevlin Park Road. After 4 miles cross Tumalo Creek and promptly stop at a parking lot on the left marked "Picnic Area Only — No Overnight Camping." Walk 100 feet past the gate. Opposite the caretaker's house turn left at the "Alder Meadows" sign and cross the meadow to a suspension footbridge across Tumalo Creek. The trail becomes clear here.

A 1990 forest fire narrowly spared the park, burning right up to this footbridge. The next half mile of trail, along the canyon's east rim, was used as the fire line. On the left are black snags; on the right, green forest. The contrast provides an interesting look at how high desert vegetation recovers from fire. Bunchgrasses have regrown from their fireproof roots. Many old ponderosa pines also have survived. These conifers' thick bark is designed to flake off during fires, relieving the trunk of heat. Older ponderosas also restrict their

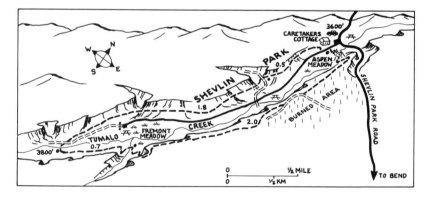

Suspension bridge over Tumalo Creek.   *Opposite: Prairie star.*

greenery to widely spaced needle clusters high off the ground, thus preventing most range fires from "crowning out."

At 0.4 mile the trail joins a dirt road. Follow the road 400 yards along the canyon rim before turning right into unburned forest on the continuation of the trail. The next portion of the trail is perhaps the most scenic of all, offering views across the creek to the canyon's far rim. At the 2-mile mark, descend steeply into an oasis-like creekside meadow among the pines. Though the popular Fremont Meadow picnic area is nearby, picnickers rarely cross Tumalo Creek to this hidden glen.

To continue on the loop, jump across a 4-foot side creek. The trail switchbacks up to the canyon rim again and then gradually descends for 0.7 mile to Tumalo Creek. A suspension bridge here washed out in 1989 and was replaced with a gangplank salvaged from a U.S. Navy ship.

Beyond Tumalo Creek the trail crosses a dirt road and contours 2.3 miles along the canyon's dry north slope, ending at the park road 100 yards short of the caretaker's house. This trailhead is identified by 2 small, signless posts.

Other Hiking Options

City parkland also extends to the north of Shevlin Park Road. To explore this wilder portion, start at Aspen Hall, a conference building in the picnic area north of the road. An undeveloped hiking route follows Tumalo Creek about 1.5 miles downstream to an irrigation canal.

33   Tumalo Falls

Easy (to South Fork Shelter)
4-mile loop
700 feet elevation gain
Open May through December
Map: Tumalo Falls (USGS)

Moderate (to Swampy Lakes)
8.4-mile loop
1300 feet elevation gain
Open June through November

Travelers who drive out from Bend to visit picturesque, 85-foot Tumalo Falls often overlook the woodsy trail network beginning here. One easy loop follows the South Fork of Tumalo Creek to a rustic shelter and returns past a seldom-visited waterfall on Bridge Creek. The walk is particularly nice in May, when forest wildflowers bloom, and in summer, as a quick escape from Central Oregon's heat. To make the hike a little more challenging, add a 2.2-mile detour up to the meadows at Swampy Lakes. Horses and mountain bikes share all of these trails.

South Fork Shelter.   *Above: Porcupine-gnawed lodgepole pines.*

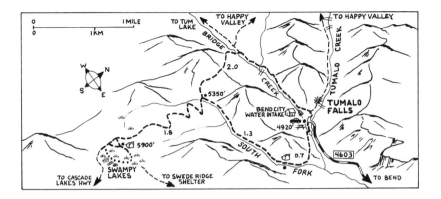

Take Galveston Street west from downtown Bend. At the end of pavement in 11 miles, turn right on gravel Road 4601, cross a one-lane bridge, and promptly turn left on gravel Road 4603 for 2.5 miles to its end at the Tumalo Falls Picnic Area. Stretch your legs by walking to the nearby viewpoint of the falls. Then return to the lower end of the parking area and begin the loop hike at the "South Fork Trail" sign.

The trail promptly crosses Bridge Creek on a footbridge and enters the Bridge Creek Burn, a 6-square-mile area regenerating from a 1979 forest fire. Though replanted with ponderosa pine in 1982, the area has regrown heavily with pungent manzanita brush. After 0.4 mile leave the burned area and begin following South Fork through a cool, mixed conifer forest with numerous wildflowers: queen's cup, star-flowered smilacina, and grass of Parnassus.

The South Fork Shelter (also known as the Tumalo Falls Shelter) makes a pleasant stop — or even a first backpack goal for hikers with children. The wood stove and substantial woodpile attest to winter use by cross-country skiers.

The trail follows the creek 1.3 miles past the shelter to a junction. If you only want to take the 4-mile loop, turn right. This route climbs over a low, forested ridge, drops to a crossing of Bridge Creek, and returns through a portion of the Bridge Creek Burn to the picnic area.

If, however, you'd like to visit Swampy Lakes, turn left. This route switchbacks up the valley's side into a drier forest of lodgepole pine. Porcupines have chewed patches of bark off some of the pines. The trail climbs 1.4 miles, levels, and then comes to a trail junction. Turn left 0.1 mile to the Swampy Lakes Shelter — which is not near the lakes. To find them, turn left at the shelter and continue 200 yards until the trail enters a large meadow. Leave the trail and follow the edge of the meadow cross-country to the right for half a mile. Watch on your left for several ponds with ducks and lilypads. There's a view of South Sister and Tumalo Mountain (Hike #52).

From here the shortest route back is to continue to the far end of the meadow, toward South Sister. Turn right at a blue ski marker on a tall pole in the grass. Walk 100 yards cross-country through the forest to a trail skirting the meadow and follow the trail to the right. Pass 2 trail junctions in the next 200 yards, keeping left to return to the switchbacking route down to South Fork. From there, return to the car via Bridge Creek.

34 Dillon and Benham Falls

Easy (to Big Eddy Falls)
4.6 miles round-trip
100 feet elevation gain
Open year-round
Map: Benham Falls (USGS)

Moderate (to Dillon Falls)
9.2 miles round-trip
300 feet elevation gain

Moderate (to Benham Falls, with shuttle)
8.4 miles one-way
400 feet elevation gain

The Deschutes River has many moods, in places flowing glassily between meadowed shores, and then churning angrily through lava canyons. This trail, just minutes from Bend, explores both humors. Since the path can be accessed at a dozen points, hikes of varying lengths are possible. The river serves as a reliable landmark throughout, keeping hikers on the right track even when the trail is muddled by primitive campsites, horse paths, and mountain bike routes.

Drive 6 miles from Bend on the Cascades Lakes Highway and turn left just before a golf course onto a gravel road signed to "Meadow Picnic Area." Drive 0.8 mile to the river and turn right for another 0.5 mile to a turnaround.

The trail starts among ponderosa pine and pungent manzanita, with views across the rugged lava that splits the river at Lava Island's rapids. At 0.5 mile reach a trail junction and turn left across a pond's dike. (The trail to the right leads up to the Inn at Seventh Mountain.) On the far end of the dike, turn left for 100 feet, then take a right-hand fork across a ditch.

In another 0.5 mile, come to the Lava Island Rock Shelter, a 4-foot cave where archeologists found evidence of 7000 years of human habitation. A few hundred yards beyond pass the Lava Island Trailhead, and despite some trail confusion

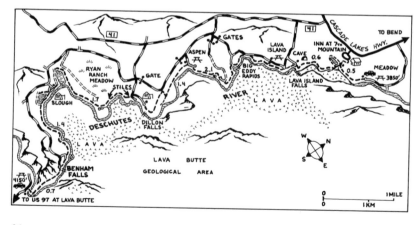

Deschutes River Trail at Lava Island.   Opposite: Grass of Parnassus.

thereafter, simply follow the riverbank for 0.6 mile to Big Eddy Falls, a half-mile series of riffles that commence with a churning chute — an ideal spot to watch river rafters flail and squeal.

Hikers with children may wish to turn back here, but hardier walkers will want to continue to Dillon Falls' more dramatic chasm. After Big Eddy Rapids the trail still hugs the riverbank, passing one dead–end jeep road, briefly following another, circumventing a cattail pond, and reaching the primitive Aspen Meadows boat launch site. From here continue 0.2 mile near the riverbank. Then the trail contours through a pine forest along the edge of a large meadow for 0.2 mile, and finally, 20 feet before the trail enters the meadow, *turn right at an inconspicuous trail junction.*

Climb a piney slope, switchback to the left at a gravel road, and follow a faint path through a tableland of rabbit brush, always keeping within 100 yards of the tableland's rimrock edge. After 0.4 mile of this pathfinding, reach the overlook of Dillon Falls, a long rapids walled with 100-foot cliffs.

To continue, walk along Dillon Falls Campground's entrance road to the boat launch junction and cross a wire fence at an unmarked stile. The trail crosses a meadow and another stile before petering out in the grass. Continue ahead between a small piney hill and a slough. Reach the riverbank again after 0.2 mile, follow a clearer tread for 0.5 mile, and then hike around the shoreline of a 10-acre lake to Slough Campground. From here circumvent a 5-acre slough of pond lilies and follow the riverbank trail 1 mile to Benham Falls' turbulent cascade. A shuttle car can be left in the parking lot here (see map for driving directions), or hikers can continue another 0.7 mile along the river to a footbridge and trailhead at the Benham Falls Picnic Area. To leave a shuttle car here, drive 10 miles south of Bend on Highway 97, turn right at the Lava Butte exit, and immediately turn left onto gravel road 9702 for 4 miles.

Other Hiking Options

If Benham Falls is your goal, a popular, shorter alternative is to park at the Benham Falls Picnic Area, cross the river on the footbridge, and walk a pleasant 0.7 mile to view the falls.

35 Newberry Lava Caves

Easy (Boyd and Skeleton Caves)
1.6 miles round-trip
200 feet elevation gain
Open year-round
Map: Kelsey Butte (USGS)

Moderate (Wind Cave)
1.2 miles round-trip
600 feet elevation gain
Open May through October

This collection of short hikes explores the chilly lava tubes riddling the flanks of Newberry Crater outside Bend. Bring one flashlight per person — and a lantern as well, if possible. And don't forget coats. Even on a hot day it's cold underground.

Newberry Crater's broad slopes are built of countless basalt lava flows. When the flows were molten the basalt was so runny that even after its surface solidified, liquid rock flowed underneath. The draining lava left long, tube-like caverns. Today, a cluster of 4 caves is accessible, the first 2 of which are hikable even by children.

Drive 4 miles south of Bend on Highway 97 and turn left on paved China Hat Road (which becomes gravel Road 18). After 9 miles turn left at the sign to Boyd Cave. Park at the turnaround and climb down the wooden staircase. The main cave extends to the left. Note the roof's *lavacicles* — stone drips caused when superheated gases long ago roared through the cave, remelting the surface rock. After 0.2 mile a rockfall obstructs the passage. By scrambling, hikers can continue another 100 feet to the cave's definitive end.

To reach the even more impressive Skeleton Cave, return to Road 18, drive east 0.5 mile, and turn left at the "Skeleton Cave" sign for 1.6 miles. Stairs lead down into the large, collapsed opening. Head left (north) along a spacious sandy-bottomed corridor often 20 feet tall and 30 feet wide. After 0.4 mile the

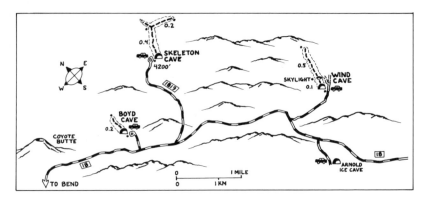

cave forks. Avoid the left fork, which promptly diminishes to a low-ceilinged squeeze; bats inhabit this cranny and deserve an undisturbed habitat. Instead take the right-hand fork, a cylindrical tube curving downhill. After 0.1 mile the floor becomes jumbled with rocks. Adequate headroom ends in another 0.1 mile, with the terminus a 100-foot scramble beyond.

Spelunkers looking for a more athletic challenge need only return to Road 18, drive another 2 miles east, and turn left at the sign for Wind Cave. This cave is floored with large, jumbled rocks, some of them wobbly. Enter only with boots, steady legs, and determination. After boulder-hopping for 0.1 mile, reach a 35-foot-tall room lit by a natural skylight. The remaining 0.5 mile of the cave consists of 5 cathedral-like halls separated by wearisome, 60-foot-tall rockpiles. Note the lines along the walls, "high-water marks" of ebbing lava flows.

A large bat colony hibernates in Wind Cave from November to late April. Do not enter the cave during this time.

The final cave is unhikable but nonetheless interesting. Return to Road 18, drive 0.6 mile east, turn right at the "Arnold Ice Cave" sign, and park after 1 mile at the end of gravel. Take a short trail down into the large, cliff-rimmed pit to the left to see Arnold Ice Cave's former entrance, now filled with solid ice. Earlier in this century a Bend company harvested summer ice blocks here.

Entrance to Boyd Cave.   Opposite: Lava drips.

36   Paulina Creek

Easy
5.6 miles round-trip
500 feet elevation gain
Open year-round
Map: Finley Butte (USGS)

Paulina Creek springs from a caldera lake high in the Newberry National Volcanic Monument, tumbles down the volcano's slopes in a series of waterfalls, and meanders across the high desert. This easy hike follows the lower, most accessible portion from the flats of Paulina Prairie to the stream's first major falls. The trip is particularly nice in very early spring or very late fall, when higher trails are closed by snow. If you're bringing children, consider shuttling a second car to the McKay Crossing trailhead, trimming the walk to just 2.8 miles one-way. Though the path is closed to motorized travel, expect to meet horses.

Turn off Highway 97 at the sign for Newberry Crater (22 miles south of Bend or 6.5 miles north of La Pine), drive 2.8 miles east on paved Road 21, turn left at Ogden Group Camp, and drive around the camp loop to the well-marked Peter Skene Ogden Trailhead.

The trail crosses glassy, swift Paulina Creek on a footbridge and heads upstream. The creek's meadowed banks form a narrow oasis here, with the dry flora of the high desert on either hand. The sagebrush-like bush is bitterbrush (*Purshia tridentata*) — a member of the rose family, as its tiny blooms in May and June reveal. The prominent trailside bunchgrass is known as "needles and thread" because of its needle-like, seed-bearing stalks and curly, thread-like basal leaves.

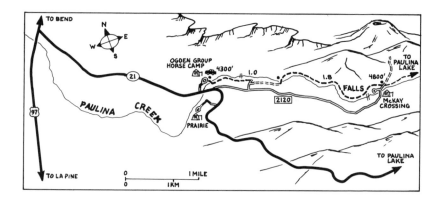

Falls near McKay Crossing.   Opposite: Ponderosa pine cone.

After 0.6 mile pass a 6-foot waterfall in a small, rocky gorge to the left. Then, 300 yards later, the trail apparently ends at a dirt road. Turn right for 50 feet to a road intersection, turn left (following yellow horseshoe-shaped markers), and walk along this road 0.2 mile to its end at the creek bank. Cross a footbridge here to the continuation of the trail.

The next half mile of trail follows the level bed of an abandoned railroad grade, used for logging early in the century. Since then, lodgepole pines have returned in force and second-growth ponderosa pines are already a proud 100 feet tall, but occasional 3-foot-thick stumps recall the earlier Central Oregon woods.

As the creek climbs it cuts deeper, at times churning and sliding through a rocky gorge. Finally come to a 15-foot waterfall at the head of a twisting rock gorge. Immediately beyond, the trail skirts the primitive campground at McKay Crossing, reaching Road 2120 near the bridge.

Other Hiking Options

The Peter Skene Ogden Trail follows Paulina Creek a total of 8.6 miles to Paulina Lake. If you'd like to explore more of it, continue past McKay Crossing 2.5 miles to a major waterfall — a 10.6-mile round-trip hike. Or, if you have two cars, leave one at the lower trailhead, drive the other to Paulina Lake, and hike the entire path downhill. Backpacking campsites are plentiful throughout.

To find the upper trailhead, turn left off paved Road 21 at the "Paulina Lake" sign just before the campground toll booth. Park at the trail sign on the left immediately after crossing the lake outlet bridge.

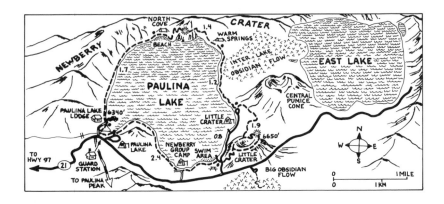

37   Paulina Lake

Easy (with shuttle to Little Crater C.G.)
4.3 miles one-way
200 feet elevation gain
Open mid-July through October
Maps: Paulina Pk., East L. (USGS)

Moderate (around lake via Little Crater)
8.4-mile loop
500 feet elevation gain

At the heart of Oregon's newest national monument, Paulina Lake has the feel of an exotic sea. Deep, azure waters lap against rocky shores. Seagulls cry. Hidden beaches beckon. But this remarkable lake is actually well over a mile above sea level, and the forested rim that walls it from the outside world is in fact the collapsed caldera of Newberry Crater, an enormous volcano. If all this fails to pique your curiosity, how about submarine hot springs, a gigantic flow of obsidian glass, and a miniature cinder cone crater?

To drive here, turn off Highway 97 at the sign for Newberry Crater (22 miles south of Bend or 6.5 miles north of La Pine) and follow paved Road 21 uphill for 13 miles. Just before the campground toll booth turn left at a "Paulina Lake" sign for 0.2 mile, and park at the Paulina Lake Lodge's log cabins — a restaurant and a rustic mercantile where gasoline can be bought and boats rented. A signboard ahead near the lakeshore marks the trail (closed to bikes and horses).

Start out along the shore in front of the lodge's rental cottages. Before long the trail enters an oddly mixed forest of lowland ponderosa pine and highland firs. Note how the older trees are flocked with glowing green *Letharia* lichen, a sure sign of clean mountain air. After 1.7 miles reach primitive North Cove Campground, accessible only by trail or boat. Here are picnic tables, an outhouse, and a fine pebble beach suitable for (chilly!) swimming.

After North Cove the path rounds a rocky headland and climbs to a viewpoint above a red cinder rockslide. Paulina Peak's jagged face looms directly across the lake, while a gap in the caldera rim to the right allows a glimpse out to cone-shaped Mt. McLoughlin and spire-topped Mt. Thielsen.

Descend to a long, meadowed beach at the undeveloped Warm Springs Campground. The offshore hot springs encourage the growth of algae here — unpleasant for swimmers but attractive to other fauna. Watch for mallards, mule deer, gray jays, and Stellar's jays. At beach's end the trail skirts the Inter Lake Obsidian Flow for 0.4 mile, passing boulders of banded volcanic glass.

At the 4.3-mile mark, reach a trailhead at the extreme north end of Little Cinder Campground. If you're hiking with children, it may be best to arrange a car shuttle to this point and call it quits. If you don't have a second car, the quickest way back is to walk 0.8 mile along the paved road through the campground and then continue 2.4 miles around the lake. But if you've got the energy for a slightly longer, more scenic route, you don't have to walk along the road at all. Here's how: when you come to the campground trailhead, turn left and hike up the steps on the unmarked Little Crater Trail. This path climbs 0.6 mile through the woods to the rim of a tiny volcano's crater. Turn left along the rim and climb to a spectacular viewpoint overlooking both Paulina and East Lakes. Continue around the rim to a junction on the far side. Turn left here and descend to the picnic area at the entrance to Little Crater Campground. Cross the road and continue along the shore 2.4 miles, following "Trail" signposts where necessary, past summer houses and campgrounds to the car.

View of Warm Springs beach and Central Pumice Cone.   Opposite: Marbled obsidian.

38 Newberry Crater Rim

Moderate (to Cinder Hill viewpoint)
5.8 miles round-trip
1000 feet elevation gain
Open August to mid-October
Map: East Lake (USGS)

The 5-mile-wide "crater" enclosing Paulina and East Lakes in the Newberry National Volcanic Monument is technically not a crater at all. It's a *caldera* — the gaping hole left when a volcano empties its insides through monumental eruptions and then collapses. Crater Lake nestles in a very similar caldera.

Hikers will appreciate a difference between Crater Lake and Newberry Crater: one has a rim *road* and the other has a rim *trail*. The hike to Cinder Hill explores a rarely visited portion of Newberry Crater's 21-mile rim trail, leading to a wide-angle view of the entire caldera.

Turn off Highway 97 at the sign for Newberry Crater (22 miles south of Bend or 6.5 miles north of La Pine) and follow the paved road 13 miles to the campground toll booth and information center at Paulina Lake. Continue another 6.2 miles, following the pavement to the extreme far end of East Lake, past the East Lake Resort to Cinder Hill Campground. In August you can drive all the way to the inconspicuous trailhead at campsite #70. After Labor Day the far end of Cinder Hill Campground is closed due to low use; in this case, park at the gate and walk 0.3 mile.

The first few hundred yards of trail have been obscured by a campground tree removal operation. Starting at the "Hiker Trail" sign beside campsite #70, follow yellow T symbols across a clearing to a trail junction in the forest. Turn left.

East Lake from Cinder Hill.   Opposite: Fragile plant growing in cinders.

The path now sets out through a fairly dull stand of small lodgepole pine, but soon begins to climb up a hidden valley. Notice how the sunny slope to the right still has dry lodgepole pines, while the shadier slope on the left is damp enough for a stand of mountain hemlock dripping with gray lichen.

After a mile the trail switchbacks up, climbing more steeply. The trail is quite clear here, so it doesn't matter that the yellow horseshoe-shaped trail markers along the way have been chewed to bits by porcupines with a taste for yellow paint.

Finally crest the ridge at a saddle with a trail junction. Alas, like almost all of the rim, this saddle is so thickly forested you only get glimpses out across the caldera. That's why you should turn right here and follow the Rim Trail 1.1 nearly level miles to Cinder Hill, a huge open slope with an unobscured view. Here you can see how half a dozen cinder cones and lava flows have split the caldera's original large lake in two.

The red cinder slope appears barren but is really a very fragile habitat for tiny, diehard flowers. Do not gouge footprints all over the slope. Stay to the upper fringe, where gnarled whitebark pines strike scenic poses. The view extends west to Mt. Thielsen's spire, Cowhorn Mountain, and Diamond Peak.

Other Hiking Options

If you'd like a longer hike and have a second car, you can continue either way around the Rim Trail. If you go clockwise, it's 4.4 miles from the Cinder Hill viewpoint to China Hat Road 21. To drive to that trailhead, return to the junction by the East Lake Resort and take the gravel road 2.2 miles to a pass. If you want to hike counterclockwise around the Rim Trail, your goal is the outlet bridge at Paulina Lake, 6.5 miles away from the trail junction in the saddle above Cinder Hill Campground.

39   Smith Rock

Easy (along river)
6.6 miles round-trip
200 feet elevation gain
Open year-round
Map: Redmond (USGS)

Moderate (across Misery Ridge)
4.1-mile loop
800 feet elevation gain

Smith Rock juts from the Central Oregon lava plains like an orange-sailed ship in the desert. Oregon's most popular rock-climbing area, this state park challenges mountaineers with 3 miles of rhyolite cliffs and Monkey Face, a 300-foot-tall natural sculpture overhanging on all sides.

Hikers can experience Smith Rock's scenic drama too. For an easy trip, walk along the aptly named Crooked River as it curls past the base of Monkey Face. For a steep shortcut back, climb a new loop beside Monkey Face across Misery Ridge to cliff-edge views of a string of Cascade snowpeaks.

The area is best in early spring, when high desert wildflowers bloom, or in winter when other trails are blocked by snow. Anytime you're rained out of a hike in the Cascades, Smith Rock is likely to be a dry alternative. Just avoid July and August when the park bakes in 100-degree heat.

To drive to the park, turn off Highway 97 at Terrebonne (6 miles north of Redmond or 20 miles south of Madras). Follow "Smith Rock State Park" signs east for 3.3 zigzagging miles to the parking area.

Walk past the restrooms to an overlook at the far end of the picnic area. Follow a gated dirt road down through an aromatic stand of tall sagebrush, cross the river bridge to a trail junction, and turn left along the riverbank. You'll soon round a bend and come to 2 side trails signed for The Dihedrals and Asterisk Pass; these climb up stairs and end at cliffs where climbers dangle, jangling their gear. Explore these side trails by hiking up the first path, turning left, and descending on the second path.

Then continue downriver, watching the plentiful bird life. Black-and-white magpies swoop from gnarled junipers. Pigeons coo in rock cracks. The eagles who hunt these birds soar from aeries high on the cliffs. At the 2-mile mark the trail rounds the tip of a peninsula and soon offers the first view ahead to Monkey Face. Look for climbers resting in the mouth cave. The trail is rough for 0.2 mile, with some scree, then passes a cave and a house-sized boulder. Here the riverside trail splits into several diffuse paths. Cross a rockslide to the balancing rocks atop ash pillars — a good turnaround point.

If you'd like to try the new shortcut back, hike to the base of Monkey Face and turn uphill on a path that climbs in long switchbacks up the ridge. The trail becomes a little vague at the top, but head right to an overlook of Monkey Face's astonishing monolith. Views extend across Central Oregon to peaks from the

Smith Rock and Crooked River.   *Opposite: Rock climber.*

Three Sisters to Mt. Hood. If you're not afraid of heights, detour briefly down to a precipice directly opposite the monkey's cave-mouth.

To complete the loop, hike 200 yards south, contouring through the sagebrush to the edge of Misery Ridge. Here 4 steep staircases have taken the misery out of the switchbacking descent to the Crooked River bridge.

Other Hiking Options

For a more challenging, 7.2-mile loop, turn *left* at the top of the trail beside Monkey Face. Bushwhack through the sagebrush along the ridgecrest 1.3 miles up to dirt Burma Road. Turn right and descend this track 1 mile. At the second switchback (where the road meets a canal) take a steep side trail down to the river. The park footbridge is a level 1-mile walk away.

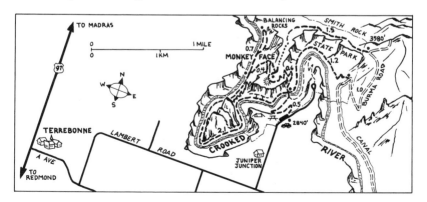

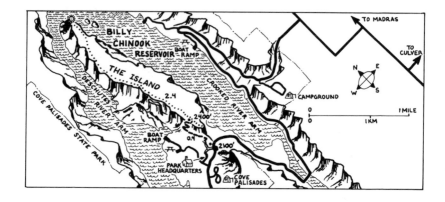

40 The Island at Cove Palisades

Moderate
5.6 miles round-trip
300 feet elevation gain
Open year-round
Map: Round Butte Dam (USGS)

If you love the desert — and have good hiking boots — this off-beat prowl through an other-worldly mesa landscape may be just the adventure for you.

When Billy Chinook Reservoir drowned the confluence of the Deschutes and Crooked Rivers, the rising waters stranded a 2-mile-long, cliff-rimmed peninsula known as The Island. Access to this lonely mesa has always been difficult; the Crooked River National Grasslands protects the flora here because it is perhaps the only area in Central Oregon never grazed by cattle or sheep. Today hikers can follow a rugged, unmarked trail up from the Cove Palisades Park road through the only gap in the mesa's rimrock. Once on top, the trail ends. But it's easy to walk the length of the mesa cross-country, discovering weird lava formations, picturesquely gnarled sagebrush, and countless clifftop viewpoints overlooking tiny waterskiers in the flooded canyons far below.

Turn west off Highway 97 at the sign for The Cove State Park (either 15 miles north of Redmond or 5 miles south of Madras) and follow similar signs on a zigzagging route west to the park's breathtaking canyon. Follow the main road down into the canyon, past a boat launch, across a suspension bridge, and up to a pass. Park at the Crooked River Petroglyph pullout on the left immediately after the pass. There is a drinking fountain here.

Walk across the paved road and follow a dirt road 100 yards past the park's ugly dump to the road's end at a compost heap. The trail begins here, switchbacking up to the right and then traversing left 0.2 mile along the base of The Island's rimrock cliffs. The path descends a bit and then climbs steeply, switchbacking up a rocky slope so rugged you have to use your hands.

At the top the trail is marked only by a metal fencepost with a small sign, "Biological Study Area. Please Cooperate in Maintaining This Study Area Undisturbed." Be sure to leave no litter and to damage no plants.

Head left along the rock-strewn sagebrush plateau. After 0.3 mile look for a strange, 40-foot-deep fissure in the ground. Half a mile beyond, the left edge of the mesa has splintered into free-standing pillars. Note how the basalt fractured hexagonally as it cooled, leaving a honeycomb of columns. Incredibly, the lava flow forming the rimrock here is the same one visible on the far side of the gorge; the Deschutes has cut its canyon since the Columbia River basalt floods buried much of Central and Eastern Oregon with lava 13 million years ago.

The north end of The Island narrows to a dramatic, windy viewpoint high above the reservoir. When returning, watch for the small metal post marking the only route down from the mesa. If you miss it, don't worry; you'll simply come to the southern tip of the mesa with a view down to your car. Backtrack 200 steps from this promontory to find the metal post and trail on the left.

Billy Chinook Reservoir from The Island.   Opposite: Columnar basalt.

The Three Sisters

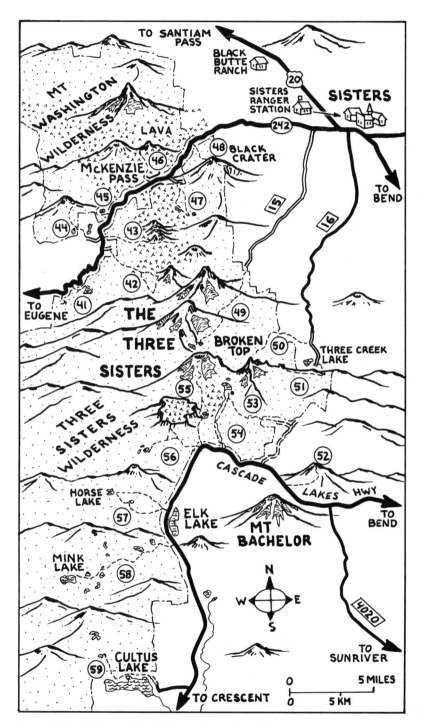

Opposite: North Sister and Middle Sister from Scott Trail junction (Hike #43).

41 Proxy Falls and Linton Lake

Easy (to Proxy Falls)
1.2-mile loop
200 feet elevation gain
Open May through November
Map: Three Sisters Wilderness (USFS)

Easy (to Linton Lake)
2.8 miles round-trip
300 feet elevation gain

The first of these 2 short walks leads across a lava flow to a pair of 100-foot waterfalls. The second trail winds through deep woods to a large lake in a steep, forest-rimmed valley.

Fire and ice have sculpted this corner of the Three Sisters Wilderness. During the Ice Age, glaciers from the Three Sisters poured down this canyon, scouring it to a deep U-shaped trough. When the ice melted some 6000 years ago, the canyon's side valleys were left hanging. Upper and Lower Proxy Falls spill over these glacier-cut cliffs. Since then, blocky basalt lava flows from cinder cones near North Sister have flooded the canyon floor, damming Linton Lake. Water seeps through the porous lava, leaving Linton Lake with no visible outlet. Likewise, the splash pool beneath Upper Proxy Falls never overflows. Apparently the water resurfaces a few miles down the canyon at the massive springs which create Lost Creek and White Branch Creek.

The Proxy Falls Trailhead is marked by an inconspicuous hiker-symbol sign on the south side of the Old McKenzie Highway between mileposts 64 and 65 (west of McKenzie Pass 13.5 miles, or 9 miles east of the Highway 126 junction). Park on the shoulder. For the loop, follow the right-hand trail up across the lava. The flow is old enough so that vine maples provide splashes of color in autumn. Nearer water the lava is overgrown with moss, twinflower, and yew trees. At a

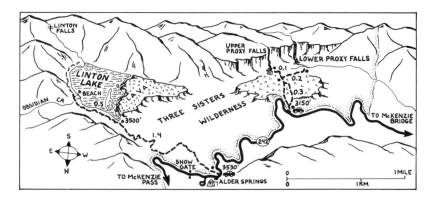

Linton Lake.   Opposite: Star moss.

trail junction keep right a few yards to a fork. Turn left to visit Upper Proxy Fall's pool. Then explore the other trail fork to Lower Proxy Fall's overlook.

To visit Linton Lake, drive east up the winding Old McKenzie Highway another 1.5 miles to a hiker-symbol sign and a small parking area on the left at Alder Springs Campground. On weekends, parking can be tight. Walk across the highway to the trailhead. This trail sets off among old-growth hemlock and Douglas fir. Vanilla leaf and Oregon grape bloom here in June. After a mile the path climbs over a lava bluff and switchbacks back down into the forest.

For years the maintained trail ended at the lake, with a rutted, boggy scramble path continuing around the left shore. In 1996, however, the Forest Service opened a better, rerouted path a few hundred feet higher up the fragile shore's steep slope. Follow this new trail half a mile around the lake to Obsidian Creek, where the path descends to a pleasant sandy peninsula with a view across the lake basin to distant Linton Falls.

42 Obsidian Trail

Difficult
12-mile loop
1800 feet elevation gain
Open mid-July through October
Map: Three Sisters Wilderness (USFS)

The Obsidian Trail leads to Sunshine, one of the most beautiful and heavily used alpine areas in Oregon. Brooks meander through the wildflower meadows nestled here between Middle Sister and Little Brother. Snowmelt tarns shimmer from plateaus strewn with black obsidian glass.

To limit crowds, the Forest Service is requiring that day hikers and campers headed here in the summer of 1996 pick up a permit in advance at the McKenzie Bridge Ranger Station. Permits will only be issued to 20 groups a day. Wilderness rangers strictly enforce a total ban on campfires. Tents are prohibited within 100 feet of trails or water. After 1996, call the McKenzie Bridge Ranger Station at (541) 822-3381 for the latest rules.

Turn off the Old McKenzie Highway 242 between mileposts 70 and 71 at the sign for Obsidian Trailhead (6.2 miles west of McKenzie Pass) and drive 0.4 mile to a maze of small parking spots. The lot was intentionally designed to limit parking. Overflow parking is 1.5 miles away at the Scott Lake road.

The trail begins at a message board at the far end of the parking loop and immediately forks. Head right, toward "White Branch Creek." The first mile of the path is dusty, through a hot forest of lodgepole pine and beargrass. After passing a side trail to Spring Lake, climb steadily through cooler woods of lichen-draped mountain hemlock and red huckleberry.

At the 3.4-mile mark, traverse up the face of a fresh, blocky lava flow to a viewpoint of Cascade snowpeaks from Mt. Jefferson to Middle Sister. Beyond the lava cross White Branch Creek to a trail junction in a wildflower meadow. The loop — and the lupine — begins here.

Follow the "Linton Meadows" pointer to the right. This route climbs a mile to a plateau of flashing obsidian chips. This black volcanic glass forms when silica-rich rhyolite lava oozes to the surface without contacting water. If rhyolite contains water it explodes upon eruption, forming frothy pumice instead.

The trail follows a brook in a meadow with western pasque flower—the early, anemone-like bloom that develops a dishmop seed head known as "old man of the mountain." At the Pacific Crest Trail junction, turn left and climb past 20-foot Obsidian Falls to a spring atop the Arrowhead Lakes' glorious alpine plateau. Pass a stunning view of North Sister and switchback down to Sunshine, a meadow beside Glacier Creek. Sunshine Shelter was demolished in the 1960s but the trail junction here is still a crossroads for wilderness traffic. Turn left to

North and Middle Sisters.   Opposite: Pasque flower seed heads.

continue the loop, following Glacier Creek steeply down to White Branch's meadow and the return route to the car.

Other Hiking Options

For a challenging 15-mile loop through the best of this area's volcanic landscape, follow the PCT north from Sunshine 2.2 miles to Collier Cone. At a rock cairn there, take a 0.4-mile side trail to the right to a breathtaking view of Collier Glacier. Then continue 1.8 miles north on the PCT, turn left on the Scott Trail for 4.9 miles (see Hike #43), and take a 0.6-mile connector trail left to the car at Obsidian Trailhead.

More difficult destinations are Linton Meadows (4 miles south of Obsidian Falls on the PCT) and the summit of Middle Sister (an arduous, but non-technical climb from Sunshine).

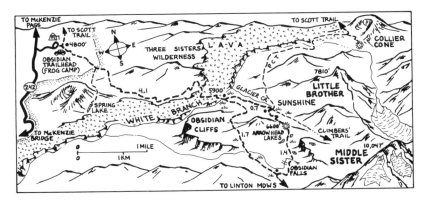

The Three Sisters from Four-In-One Cone.   Opposite: Dead whitebark pines.

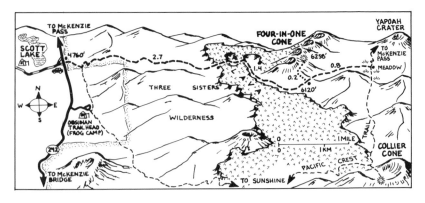

43   Four-In-One Cone

Moderate
8.6 miles round-trip
1500 feet elevation gain
Open: mid-July through October
Map: Three Sisters Wilderness
    (USFS)

When Captain Felix Scott led the first wagon train through the McKenzie Pass area in 1862, he blazed a sinuous route across an alien volcanic landscape of cinder cones and lava flows at the base of North Sister. This hike traces his footsteps, following the Scott Trail to a viewpoint atop the crater rim of 4 connected cinder cones. If you have the energy to hike 0.8 mile further, you can picnic in a meadow with one of Oregon's best lupine displays.

Take the Old McKenzie Highway 242 and park at the Scott Lake turnoff between mileposts 71 and 72 (west of McKenzie Pass 5.6 miles). The trail starts at a hiker-symbol sign on the south side of the highway.

After 0.2 mile pass a connector trail on the right to Obsidian Trailhead. Go straight and begin to climb, switchbacking up from a dry forest of lodgepole pine and beargrass to moister mountain hemlock woods. At the 2.7-mile mark, cross a 200-yard jumble of barren, blocky lava to a forested "island" entirely surrounded by the basalt flows. The trail then crosses another 100 yards of lava and climbs gradually for 1.4 miles along the sandy fringe between the woods and the lava flow's rugged wall.

The trail finally crests in a broad cinder barrens. North Sister dominates the horizon to the right; Four-In-One Cone is the cinder pile to the left. Boots are required for the short, steep cross-country climb up Four-In-One Cone because the cinder scree is loose and jagged. Once you're on top the crater rim, you can walk as far as you like along the summit of the 4 contiguous cones, with top-of-the-world views of half a dozen Cascade peaks.

Note how lava flows have breached each of the 4 craters. Cinder cones form when a blip of magma rises to the surface. An initial violent eruption spews cinders, with prevailing western winds usually building the cone highest on the east rim. The cinder cone dies once the magma has released its volatile gases, but a quieter basalt flow then typically pours from the cone's base.

To lunch in greener pastures, continue on the Scott Trail a relatively level 0.8 mile to a delightful meadow at the Pacific Crest Trail junction. Lupine blooms profusely here from mid-July through August.

Other Hiking Options

To extend this hike to a challenging 15-mile loop, return via the PCT and the Obsidian Trail (see Hike #42).

44   Benson Lake

Easy (to Benson Lake)
2.8 miles round-trip
400 feet elevation gain
Open July through October
Map: Mt. Washington Wilderness (USFS)

Moderate (to Scott Mountain)
10.8 miles round-trip
1300 feet elevation gain
Open mid-July through October

The hike to beautifully blue, cliff-rimmed Benson Lake is short enough for children, yet can be lengthened if you'd like more exercise. Just 1.1 miles further up the trail you can explore the somewhat less heavily visited Tenas Lakes — half a dozen swimmable pools scattered among huckleberry meadows and forests. Or you can continue another 1.5 miles to the wildflowers and mountain views at Scott Mountain's former lookout site. Backpackers should bring a permit and cannot use campfires within 100 feet of lakes or trails.

Start by driving the Old McKenzie Highway to the Scott Lake turnoff between mileposts 71 and 72 (west of McKenzie Pass 5.6 miles). Follow Road 260 for 1.5 miles to its end at a gravel pit and turnaround. The Benson Trail climbs steadily through a mixed lodgepole pine forest graced by *Pedicularis,* a dainty stalk of beak-shaped blooms with the unbecoming common name of lousewort. After 1 mile, cross the (usually dry) outlet creek of Benson Lake. When the trail finally crests a ridge, take a side trail left to the lakeshore. Here dragonflies zoom, small fish jump, and northern toads lurk — particularly during the first half of July when mosquitoes, their favorite prey, are common.

There is no developed trail around Benson Lake, but routes for exploration abound. For starters, take a fishermen's path to the left, cross the lake's outlet, and scramble up a rock ridge to a viewpoint overlooking the lake, 2 of the Three Sisters, and Mount Scott. Note how the bedrock here has been rounded and

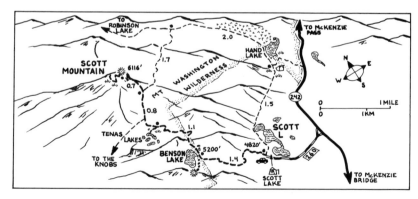

Benson Lake with Scott Mountain on horizon.   Opposite: Northern toad.

smoothed by the same Ice Age glaciers that carved the lake's basin.

For a longer hike, return to the main trail, continue 1.1 miles, and take a side trail left to the Tenas Lakes. *Tenas* means "small" in Chinook jargon, the old trade language of the Northwest Indians. The first lake is actually the size of a golf fairway, with cliffs at one end. Hike around it to look for several smaller lakes on the far side. Huckleberries ripen here in August.

If Scott Mountain is your target, continue on the main trail 1.5 miles past the Tenas Lakes junction. This path aims straight for the red, barren peak, but then banks around the mountain and switchbacks up through meadows on the far side, trading cinders for cat's ears. The summit, where a lookout once stood, provides an aerial view of the entire hike's route and half a dozen Cascade peaks.

Other Hiking Options

It's only half a mile longer to return from Scott Mountain via Hand Lake, making a delightful loop on a less-crowded trail. The long abandoned 1.7-mile connecting path between Scott Mountain and the Hand Lake Trail will be rebuilt in the summer of 1996 to make this loop easier, although trail signs probably won't be posted for the reconstructed section until 1997.

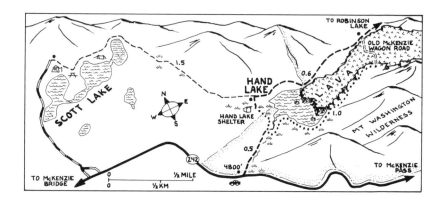

45   Hand Lake Shelter

Easy
2.2-mile loop
200 feet elevation gain
Open July through October
Map: Mt. Washington Wilderness (USFS)

If you have but one hour to spend in the Wilderness consider investing it here, for this short walk provides as much interest as a trek. In just 2.2 miles you'll pass wildflower meadows, mountain views, a rustic shelter, a lake, a lava flow, and a historic portion of the old McKenzie Wagon Road. There's even a short (but safe) trailless section to add a touch of adventure.

The trail begins at the paved McKenzie Highway 242, but the trailhead is so poorly marked it's easy to miss. Between mileposts 72 and 73 (west of McKenzie Pass 4.5 miles), watch for a wooden message board beside a meadow on the north side of the highway. The only parking area is a narrow pullout on the opposite shoulder.

The trail follows the left edge of the meadow along Hand Lake's (sometimes dry) outlet creek. This meadow is a veritable herbarium of alpine blooms from mid-July to mid-August. If you forgot a flower guidebook, identify them by color: blue lupine, purple larkspur, pink spirea, red paintbrush, yellow buttercups, and pearly everlasting.

The trail grows faint when the meadow widens, revealing a view across Hand Lake to Mt. Washington's spire. Keep left around the meadow's edge to find the 3-sided shelter. Then follow the path directly across the meadow and up a wooded slope to a trail junction. Turn right, following the "Robinson Lake" pointer. After 0.5 mile, when the trail reaches the sandy edge of a lava flow, watch for the unmarked wagon road cutting across the lava to the right. The abandoned roadway is perfectly level and 15 feet wide, but so old that a few struggling plants have had time to take root. Pioneer John Craig arduously chipped this route from the lava around 1871 as a shortcut from the Willamette Valley to Central Oregon's grazing lands.

Follow the roadbed across the lava and turn right, following the sandy margin between the lava and the forest back down to Hand Lake. Though there is no trail here, the lake's water level drops in summer, leaving a wide, hikable beach. Go around the lake to the outlet, walk left along this creek until it narrows enough to be crossable, and then continue around the lake meadows to the outlet creek and the trail back to the car.

Hand Lake, bordered by a lava flow.   Opposite: Hand Lake Shelter.

46   Little Belknap Crater

Moderate
5.2 miles round-trip
1100 feet elevation gain
Open mid-July through October
Map: Mt. Washington Wilderness (USFS)

Much of the raw-looking lava at McKenzie Pass comes from Belknap Crater and its dark twin, Little Belknap. Both mountains keep a low profile among the High Cascades' peaks, yet on average they've erupted every 1000 years since the Ice Age.

This hike along the Pacific Crest Trail follows a lava flow to its source in a throat-shaped cave atop Little Belknap. Along the way the route passes lava bombs, pressure ridges, and forested islands left in the aftermath of the eruption.

Tennis shoes won't do on this jagged lava, and even hiking boots suffer. Although this section of the Pacific Crest Trail has been dynamited to an even grade, the cinders still cut soles like glass.

Drive Highway 242 to McKenzie Pass. Half a mile west of the Dee Wright Observatory pull off at a parking area identified only by a brown hiker-symbol sign.

At first the trail's tread is not clear in the sand and dust of this sparse pine forest. Walk to the message board and head left past the "Mt. Washington Wilderness" sign. Climb 0.4 mile along the edge of an "island" surrounded by lava, then cross the blocky flow for 100 yards to the second "island" — another hill that succeeded in diverting the liquid basalt. Notice how the sunny south slope of the hill has dry manzanita and ponderosa pine, while the cooler north slope is damp enough to support huckleberry and true fir.

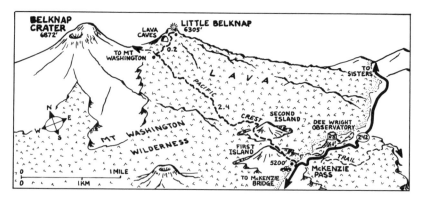

Belknap Crater from inside Little Belknap's lava caves.   *Opposite: Lava bomb.*

At the 0.8-mile mark the trail climbs onto the lava for good. Why is the flow so rugged? After the surface solidified, liquid basalt flowed on underneath the crust, buckling up pressure ridges and leaving caves that often collapsed. Since then, only a few intrepid whitebark pines and penstemons have managed to take root.

Views improve of North and Middle Sister as you climb. Ahead is Belknap Crater's red cone, whose eruption blanketed 100 square miles with ash. Blobs of molten rock were thrown high into the air, solidifying in teardrop shapes — the lava "bombs" along the slope.

Near the trail's crest, a rock cairn with a pole marks the junction to Little Belknap. Turn right and follow the path up to the summit parapet. The last 50 feet are a steep scramble to a viewpoint of peaks from Mt. Jefferson to Broken Top.

On the way back down to the trail junction explore the lava caves — actually, 3 short remnants of a single collapsed tube. Since the caves offer the only shade on this hike, they make tempting lunch spots. The uppermost cave, 50 feet north of the path, has a 40-foot-deep throat with snow at the bottom; don't fall in! Further down the trail, walk through the middle cave's culvert-like tube. The lowest cave, just south of the trail, is a low-ceilinged bunker.

Other Hiking Options

For a slightly better view, scramble up Belknap Crater. Continue north on the PCT until it leaves the lava, then head cross-country to the left, traversing to the cinder cone's less-steep northern slope. Total distance from the trailhead: 4 miles.

47   Matthieu Lakes

Easy
6-mile loop
800 feet elevation gain
Open mid-July through October
Map: Three Sisters Wilderness (USFS)

The 2 Matthieu Lakes seem worlds apart — one in a windswept pass with mountain views and the other in a deep forest sheltered by a craggy lava flow. Visit both on this easy loop along a heavily used portion of the Pacific Crest Trail.

A mile east of McKenzie Pass, turn off Highway 242 at a sign for Lava Camp Lake. Follow this cinder road 0.3 mile, then turn right to the Pacific Crest Trailhead parking area. Horse hooves have churned the Matthieu Lakes loop to deep dust.

Start on the path signed to the "P.C.N.S.T." Despite the sign's estimate of half a mile, the Pacific Crest Trail junction is only 0.2 mile away, at the edge of a lava flow. Turn left there for 0.7 mile to a junction marking the start of the loop.

Go left at this junction toward South Matthieu Lake. The PCT gradually climbs along a forested slope through ever-larger openings of bracken and red cinders. Views improve as you go. Ahead are glimpses of North and Middle Sister. Behind are spire-topped Mt. Washington and distant, snowy Mt. Jefferson. Far below in the forest is blue North Matthieu Lake.

At the 2.8-mile mark, crest a barren ridge shoulder with the best views of all. Notice the *lava bombs* scattered among the cinders here. These teardrop-shaped rocks — some as small as footballs, others as large as bears — were blown out of cinder cones in molten form and solidified in flight.

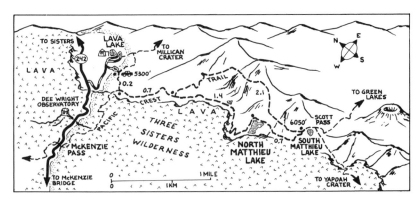

North Sister from South Matthieu Lake.   Opposite: Gnarled log by lake.

Continue across a black cinder field to South Matthieu Lake, set in Scott Pass like a gem in a ring. If you're backpacking, remember that campfires are banned in the lake area. Tents are only allowed in approved sites marked by a post, and these few sites fill fast with PCT travelers.

To continue the loop, hike back 100 yards to a trail junction sign for North Matthieu Lake. This dusty downhill route, a portion of the old Oregon Skyline Trail, descends 0.7 mile to this larger lake in a forest enlivened by cute golden-mantled ground squirrels. Here, too, permissable campsites are designated by posts. The trail follows the lakeshore to the outlet, switchbacks down through forest, and then follows the edge of a lava flow back to the PCT.

Other Hiking Options

To extend this hike, continue 2.5 miles past South Matthieu Lake on the PCT. You'll cross an impressive lava flow, contour about Yapoah Crater (the cinder cone that produced the lava), and reach a huge meadow of lupine at the Scott Trail junction (see Hike #43).

North Sister from Black Crater.   Opposite: Curled mountain hemlock twigs.

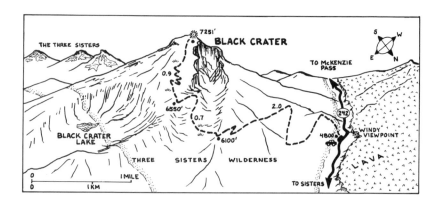

48   Black Crater

Difficult
7.2 miles round-trip
2500 feet elevation gain
Open mid-July to late October
Map: Three Sisters Wilderness
(USFS)

Ice, more than fire, built the craters of this monumental cinder cone. Ice Age glaciers scooped out one bowl for Black Crater Lake and gouged a second, higher chasm that left the peak's summit teetering atop a 500-foot cliff.

The steep trail to Black Crater's former lookout site demands stamina, but offers Central Oregon's best view of the Three Sisters and the McKenzie Pass lava flows.

The trailhead alongside Highway 242 is a clearly marked pullout located 3.5 miles east of McKenzie Pass or 11 miles west of Sisters. The path climbs steeply 0.1 to the Wilderness boundary, but then settles in to a long, steady climb amid lodgepole pine and mountain hemlock.

At the 2-mile mark, crest a ridge shoulder and traverse the undulating valley carved by a glacier. Blue and yellow wildflowers brighten meadowed depressions here. Then climb through forest again to another ridge shoulder and enter open alpine country on the butte's east flank. Soon, views open up across Central Oregon to the town of Sisters, Black Butte Ranch, and even Mt. Hood.

The path switchbacks up into the zone of dwarfed, weather-blasted pines known to alpinists as *krummholz* — German for crooked wood. In fact, the whitebark pines here are of a species that only grows above 6000 feet. To withstand winter winds, these trees developed limbs so flexible they can literally be tied in knots.

Finally the trail crosses an eerie, barren plateau of black cinders to the summit's 30-foot crag. The lookout once stood on a flattened spot nearly overhanging the crater cliffs. The trail continues several hundred yards past the summit before dying out, but the view at the top is best. To the west, black lava flows appear to have oozed like molasses from Little Belknap (Hike #46) and Yapoah Crater, leaving a dozen forested "islands" marooned in rock. The pinnacles of North Sister and Mt. Washington seem close enough to touch.

Other Hiking Options
Black Crater Lake is not visible from any point of the trail, but adventurers with a map and compass can hike cross-country 0.2 mile to an overlook of the lake's bowl-shaped valley. Leave the trail at the 6550-foot ridgecrest and contour south to the valley rim.

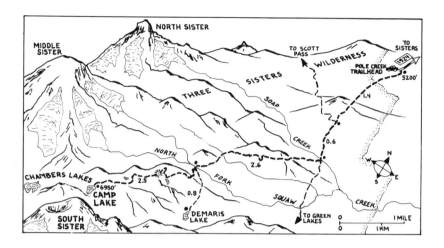

49   Chambers Lakes

Difficult (to Camp Lake)
14.2 miles round-trip
1800 feet elevation gain
Open August to mid-October
Map: Three Sisters Wilderness (USFS)

The heather ridges around Camp Lake are an alpine wonderland, set smack between towering South Sister and the glaciers of Middle Sister. Wind-sculpted pines cling to crags in scenic poses. Miniature wildflowers turn brilliant blooms to the sun. Icebergs drift in blue waters. The sky seems full of Oregon's most beautiful mountains.

But good things don't come easy. And the price of admission here is more than merely a long, uphill hike — it's a hike that starts with 4.6 miserably dusty, viewless miles. To find the trailhead, drive 1.4 miles west of Sisters on Highway 242 and turn left onto gravel Road 15 for 10.5 miles, following frequent signs for the Pole Creek Trailhead. At the end of the improved road, park at an undeveloped campground distinguished only by an outhouse. The trail begins at a prominent message board on the left.

The path climbs gradually for 1.4 miles to a junction. Turn left for 0.6 mile to Soap Creek, a welcome oasis in this dry lodgepole pine forest. Note the pink monkeyflower on the splashing creek's banks. Cross on a log footbridge to

Camp Lake and South Sister.   Opposite: Boulder split by ice expansion.

another trail junction. Keep right toward Chambers Lakes and climb more steeply into cooler, lichen-draped mountain hemlock woods.

After 2.6 miles reach Squaw Creek's roaring North Fork and the first clear view of massive Middle Sister. Squaw Creek is milky with rock silt from the peak's Diller Glacier. Cross the stream as best you can on precarious logs and slippery rocks. At a trail junction on the far bank, follow the "Camp Lake" pointer up to the right. This path switchbacks to an alpine ridgecrest with views of all Three Sisters and Broken Top. Camp Lake, the first and most accessible of the Chambers Lakes, is 2 miles along this enchanting ridge.

Despite Camp Lake's name, it's a chilly spot for an overnight stay. There's no shelter from the almost constant winds, and campfires are banned within half a mile of any of the Chambers Lakes. As everywhere in the Three Sisters Wilderness, tenters must bring permits and should locate more than 100 feet from trails or water.

Other Hiking Options

Demaris Lake is a somewhat closer goal. Though less spectacular, this lake's a good choice on days when wind or threatening weather make the Chambers Lakes uninviting. A sign at the North Fork of Squaw Creek indicates the 0.8-mile side trail. Round-trip distance from the Pole Creek Trailhead is 10.8 miles.

50   Park Meadow

Moderate (to Park Meadow)
9.8 miles round-trip
700 feet elevation gain
Open mid-July to early November
Map: Three Sisters Wilderness (USFS)

Difficult (to Golden Lake)
13.2 miles round-trip
1200 feet elevation gain
Open late July through October

Long-time outdoorsmen often have a "secret spot" in the wilderness — an alpine lakelet or a hidden wildflower meadow whose beauty they'll gladly describe in glowing terms. But ask them just *where* this paradise is and they'll only smile.

Many of these secret spots are hidden on the north flank of Broken Top. And the real reason tenderfeet aren't here is not the oath of silence but rather the difficulty of the hike. Park Meadow, the gateway to this wonderland, is nearly 5 miles along a tedious, dusty trail. Golden Lake, with a backdrop of 4 glacier-clad mountains, is another 1.7 miles — much of it utterly trailless.

Drive to downtown Sisters and turn south on Elm Street at the sign for Three Creek Lake. Follow this road for 14 paved miles, continue 0.3 mile on gravel, and park near a large sign for the Park Meadow Trailhead. The sign points right, up a very rugged 4-wheel-drive access road. This rutted track will be converted to trail as soon as a more upscale parking area is built here — perhaps by 1993. In the meantime it's probably still easiest on your car to park and walk along the dirt road 1.2 miles to the old trailhead at the end of a turnaround.

After this second trailhead the path is still 6 feet wide, churned to dust by horse hooves. But it's not a strenuous route; the round trip has 700 feet of cumulative elevation gain only because of very gradual downs and ups.

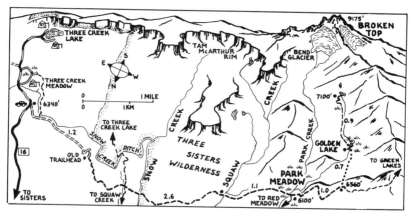

Golden Lake. Opposite: Creek below Broken Top.

Beyond the old trailhead 0.8 mile, cross an unnamed creeklet and continue straight to the Wilderness boundary at 10-foot-wide Soap Creek. Another 1.5 miles through dry lodgepole pine forest brings you to the footbridge over Squaw Creek, a mossy stream banked with clumps of beautiful pink monkeyflower.

From this oasis it's just 1 mile to the edge of Park Meadow and the first views of Broken Top, South Sister, and North Sister. Brilliant blue, cup-shaped gentians bloom in the grass here each August. Camping is discouraged in the meadow itself; overnighters should seek less fragile sites in the woods. As always in this Wilderness, permits are required and campsites should be over 100 feet from trails or water.

Only experienced hikers with map-and-compass skills should attempt to continue to Golden Lake. Cross Park Creek and immediately head left at a trail intersection, following the "Green Lakes" pointer. This path climbs 0.4 mile to a sharp switchback to the right, continues another 0.2 mile to a major, ridge-end curve to the left, and then follows the broad ridgecrest 0.3 mile to a glimpse of Broken Top's peak over a low rise to the left. Watch for a small rock cairn beside the trail.

At this point leave the trail and contour due south toward Broken Top through level, meadowed openings for 0.7 mile to the lake. If you hit a creek, follow it right to the lake. If you come to huge meadows backed by a 500-foot-tall ridge, follow the meadows left to the lake. If you insist on backpacking here, hide your tent well back in the woods.

Now here's the real secret: a small, steep trail begins at the waterfall behind Golden Lake and leads 0.9 mile up the meadowed creek to 2 beautiful, timberline tarns.

51 Tam McArthur Rim

Moderate
5 miles round-trip
1200 feet elevation gain
Open August to mid-October
Map: Three Sisters Wilderness (USFS)

Surrounded by sheer, 500-foot cliffs, the viewpoint on the edge of Tam McArthur Rim is an almost aerial overlook of the Three Sisters. Even in August a few patches of snow remain among the struggling trees and wildflowers of the rim's tablelands. Although hiking to the rim of this enormous fault scarp is not difficult, you arrive at an elevation greater than that of many Oregon mountains. Lewis ("Tam") A. McArthur was secretary of the Oregon Geographic Names Board from 1916 to 1949.

To start the hike, drive to downtown Sisters and turn south on Elm Street at the sign for Three Creek Lake. Follow Elm Street and its successor, Road 16, for 15.7 miles. After 1.7 miles of gravel, notice the trailhead sign on the left, opposite the entrance road to Driftwood Campground. Park at a lot 100 feet down the campground road and walk back to the trail.

The path climbs steeply 0.2 mile, levels off for a bit, and then climbs hard again up to the rim's plateau. Notice how porcupines have gnawed patches of bark off some of the pines. These mostly nocturnal, spiny rodents can also subsist on lupine, though it causes selenium poisoning in other mammals.

The trail climbs gradually for half a mile across the rim's tilted tableland before views begin to unfold. To the north, look for (left to right) Belknap Crater, Mt. Washington, Three Fingered Jack, Mt. Jefferson, Mt. Hood, and the tip of Mt. Adams.

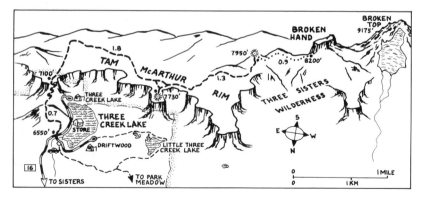

The wildflowers of this sandy plateau grow in scattered clumps to preserve moisture and to fight the winds. The bright purple trumpets are penstemon. The clumps of yellow balls are sulfur plant. And the off-white, fuzzy flowers are dirty socks — source of a suspicious odor wafting across the hot sand.

Finally, at an unmarked fork, take the smaller right-hand path 200 yards along the rim to the cliff-edge viewpoint. Three Creek Lake and its cousin, Little Three Creek Lake, are over 1000 feet below. To the east, sunlight glints off metal roofs in Bend and Sisters. To the south is snowy Mt. Bachelor, striped with ski slopes.

Other Hiking Options

If you have energy left after reaching the cliff-edge viewpoint, invest it in a relatively level 1.3-mile continuation of this hike along Tam McArthur Rim. Return to the main trail and head west toward Broken Top. After a mile of sandy, alpine country, climb a snowfield and turn left up what appears to be a small red cinder cone — but which is in fact a ridge end. Stop at the ridgecrest amid a scattering of drop-shaped lava bombs, and admire the view here stretching south to Mt. Thielsen.

It's possible to continue even further toward Broken Top, but the trail becomes faint and ends altogether at the dangerous slopes of Broken Hand.

Broken Top from Tam McArthur Rim.   Opposite: Snow-bent lodgepole pine.

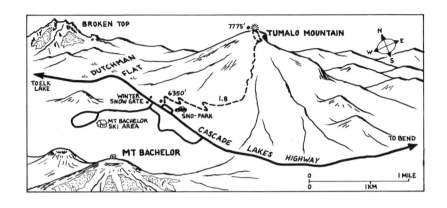

Summit of Tumalo Mountain.   Opposite: View of South Sister.

52 Tumalo Mountain

Moderate
3.6 miles round-trip
1200 feet elevation gain
Open mid-July to mid-October
Map: Three Sisters Wilderness
(USFS)

Each summer thousands of tourists ride a chairlift to the summit of Mount Bachelor for a view of the Three Sisters. But you can hike up Tumalo Mountain in an hour and get virtually the same view for free. Even better, Tumalo Mountain has no unsightly chairlifts and no throngs of tourists.

Drive 20 miles west of Bend on the Cascades Lakes Highway. Half a mile after the first Mt. Bachelor Ski Area exit, pull off into a parking area on the right signed for the Tumalo Mountain Trailhead. In winter this is the Dutchman Flat sno-park.

The trail begins at the far end of the parking area and climbs steadily through an open forest of mountain hemlock, true fir, and lupine. Meadowed openings allow glimpses of Mt. Bachelor's snowy side.

Tumalo Mountain and Mt. Bachelor are cinder cones — gigantic heaps of volcanic shrapnel. Though geologically fresh, they're both old enough to have been bitten by glaciers. Mt. Bachelor is the least damaged; it must have been so smoothly conical before the Ice Age that snow had few places to compact into ice. Tumalo Mountain, on the other hand, probably had a crater that allowed snow to collect. Under the weight of ice, the crater became a glacial cirque, leading to the destruction of the cone's entire northeast quarter.

At the trail's 1-mile mark, views begin opening up across Central Oregon to Sunriver's distant meadow. The trail climbs past gnarled whitebark pines, heads more steeply up a red cinder slope, and finally reaches the summit's long, tilted plain. Because the few struggling plants of this alpine cinder field could easily be damaged by off-trail hiking, approved paths have been clearly outlined with red cinder rocks.

On a cliff edge to the right, notice the concrete foundations of the erstwhile lookout tower. The view here extends across the Swampy Lakes' meadow (Hike #33) and the seemingly barren valleys of the 1979 Bridge Creek Burn to the rooftops of Bend.

Follow a path along the cliff edge 200 yards to the mountain's highest point. In the forests below are Dutchman Flat and Sparks Lake. And rising above them are the peaks of fame: snowy South Sister and Broken Top.

53 Green Lakes via Crater Ditch

Moderate
9.6 miles round-trip
500 feet elevation loss
Open August to mid-October
Map: Three Sisters Wilderness (USFS)

The 3 green lakes in this famed alpine basin reflect South Sister on one side and Broken Top on the other. The picturesque valley also features a glassy lava flow, wildflower meadows, gigantic springs, and a waterfall. But beauty has brought crowds, and crowds have brought restrictions. Several overused lakeshore areas are roped off for restoration. Campfires are banned. Backpackers must bring permits and should tent more than 100 feet from water or trails. To avoid the largest crowds, skip August weekends.

This trail to the Green Lakes is quieter and less steep than the Fall Creek route (Hike #54), and it has better mountain views. Road access, however, is poor.

Drive the Cascade Lakes Highway west of Bend 22 miles. Two miles beyond the Mt. Bachelor Ski Area, turn right at a sign for Todd Lake Campground. Follow gravel Road 370 half a mile to the campground parking lot and continue on what becomes a steep, miserably rutted dirt road. The route is passable for passenger cars, but demands both caution and courage. After 3.5 arduous miles, turn left at a large "Trailhead" sign and follow this side road 1.3 miles to its end.

The trail follows a barricaded dirt road for 200 yards, then turns left onto a friendlier tread at a sign for Green Lakes. After half a mile, enter a flower-filled meadow overtowered by Broken Top's cliffs. From here Broken Top offers a remarkable cut-away view of a composite volcano. The red, yellow, and black stripes are layers of red cinders, yellow ash, and black lava that built the peak into a smooth-sided cone. Explosions similar to those at Mt. St. Helens later destroyed the cone's symmetry, hurling 8-foot lava bombs across Central Oregon and burying the entire Bend area under 20 to 50 feet of debris.

At the 1-mile mark cross an irrigation ditch that diverts most of Crater Creek into the Tumalo Creek drainage for use by the Tumalo Irrigation District. The main trail continues straight and 50 yards later crosses the unchanneled remnants of Crater Creek.

The trail then contours around Broken Top, with views across Sparks, Hosmer, and Lava Lakes. On the horizon are snowy Diamond Peak and distant, pointy-topped Mt. Thielsen. Finally the path heads straight for South Sister and drops into the Green Lakes Basin.

Perhaps the best way to explore the valley is with an optional 3.1-mile loop. When you reach the first lake, turn right on an unmarked trail. Skirt the right-hand shore of this lake and the next, larger lake, passing picture-postcard

Broken Top from Crater Creek meadow.   Opposite: Obsidian boulder at Green Lakes.

views of South Sister. After crossing a footbridge over the third lake's outlet creek, leave the trail and head cross-country to the left around the largest lake. Stay on the cinder plain; the lakeshore meadows are swampy here. Hike along the far western edge of the valley floor, passing enormous springs, a milky outwash creek from Lewis Glacier, and a blocky lava flow of shiny obsidian. To complete the loop, cross Fall Creek on narrow, tippy logs and go straight.

Other Hiking Options

With a car shuttle you can make this trip all downhill. After hiking to Green Lakes via Crater Ditch, continue 4.2 miles down the Fall Creek Trail (Hike #54) to the Cascade Lakes Highway.

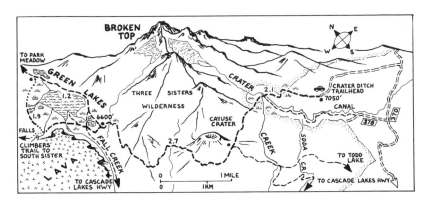

54 Green Lakes via Fall Creek

Moderate
8.8 miles round-trip
1100 feet elevation gain
Open mid-July through October
Map: Three Sisters Wilderness (USFS)

This classic route to the famous alpine basin of the Green Lakes is a little shorter and more accessible than the less-used Crater Ditch Trail (Hike #53). The path up Fall Creek has other charms as well, for it leads past a string of waterfalls and through a strangely idyllic canyon walled by an enormous lava flow. Although the trail is dusty from extremely heavy use, you can avoid the worst traffic by skipping August weekends.

Take the Cascade Lakes Highway 25 miles west of Bend (4.5 miles past the Mt. Bachelor Ski Area) and turn right at a sign for the Green Lakes Trailhead. The path starts at the end of the parking loop on the left.

After 200 yards the trail crosses swift, glassy Fall Creek on a footbridge. Half a mile beyond is the first waterfall, a 25-foot-wide curtain of water. But don't spend all your time here. Just 100 yards upstream is another major cataract. In fact, the creek puts on a trailside performance for the next 1.5 miles, tumbling through chutes, juggling over boulders, and falling headlong into pools.

After a trail splits off toward Moraine Lake on the left, cross Fall Creek again on a footbridge in a meadow with glimpses ahead to South Sister and Broken Top. Blue lupine, yellow composites, and pink monkeyflower bloom here in August.

Then the trail climbs through the woods for a mile before returning to Fall Creek in an eerie meadow flanked by a massive lava flow on the left. This wall

#54

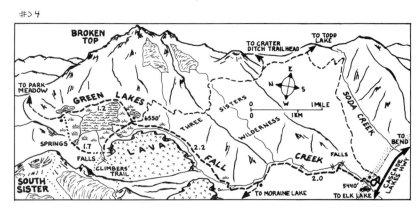

South Sister from the largest Green Lake.   Opposite: Lava flow beside Fall Creek.

of blocky obsidian created the Green Lakes Basin thousands of years ago by damming Fall Creek. Since then, sediment has washed down from the mountains on either side, filling most of the basin and splitting the original single lake into 3 parts.

The obsidian flow itself is a sign of South Sister's old age. Young volcanoes typically spew cinders and pour out fluid basalt lava. As the volcano ages, its magma often becomes richer in silica, the mineral in glass. Silica makes the magma so thick that lava can clog up the volcano's vent, causing a Mt. St. Helens-style explosion. If that happens, the silica-rich magma froths out as pumice or shatters into ash. If the volcano is dying quietly, however, the silica may ooze out as obsidian — blocks of shiny glass.

Finally reach a 4-way trail junction just before the lakes. To prowl the lake basin on an optional 2.9-mile loop, continue straight. See Hike #53 for a description of this loop.

The fragile alpine meadows around the Green Lakes have been so severely overused that restrictions are necessary. Many lakeshores are closed to entry as restoration areas. Campfires are banned throughout the entire basin. Overnighters must bring permits and should not camp within 100 feet of any trail or water source.

Other Hiking Options

If you'd like to return a different way to your car — and if you don't mind adding 3.1 scenic miles to the day's walk — take the Crater Ditch Trail east from the 4-way trail junction at the Green Lakes. After 2.8 miles turn right at a sign for the Fall Creek Trailhead and follow the Soda Creek Trail 4.5 miles down to the parking area.

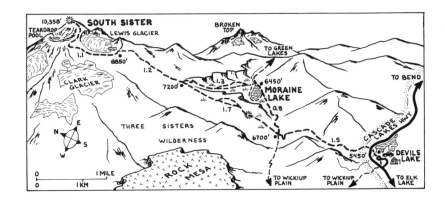

55 Moraine Lake and South Sister

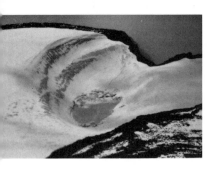

Moderate (to Moraine Lake)
6.8-mile loop
2000 feet elevation gain
Open August to mid-October
Map: Three Sisters Wilderness (USFS)

Very Difficult (to summit of South Sister)
11 miles round-trip
4900 feet elevation gain

Oregon's third tallest peak has a path to its top. Admittedly, the trail up South Sister is exceedingly steep, long, and rugged, but no technical climbing skills are required and the rewards are great. From the summit — a broad, snowy crater with a small lake — you can see half the state.

If this sounds too demanding, here's a secret: the loop to Moraine Lake, halfway up the mountain, is just as picturesque. This lower hike avoids the final trudge up cinder scree, yet still offers views 100 miles south to Mt. McLoughlin. Moraine Lake itself, a sandy-shored reflecting pool, is set in a dramatic alpine valley strewn with wildflowers and pumice. What's more, the weather's better here. The summit often generates its own wisp of clouds — a scenic feature when viewed from below, but a nuisance at the top.

To start these popular hikes, drive 27 miles west of Bend on the Cascade Lakes Highway. Beyond the Mt. Bachelor Ski Area 6.5 miles, turn left at Devils Lake Campground. Park at the end of the campground loop at the sign for the South Sister Climbers' Trail.

The path crosses a footbridge over glassy Tyee Creek, then crosses the highway and climbs steeply through a dense mountain hemlock forest. At the 1.5-mile mark the path switchbacks sharply up a dry gulch and suddenly emerges from the forest at the edge of a vast, sandy plateau. South Sister and

Broken Top loom ahead. Signs at a 4-way trail junction here indicate Moraine Lake is to the right — but to take the recommended, scenic loop to Moraine Lake, follow the "South Sister" pointer straight ahead.

This portion of the hike is a lark — strolling up the open tableland, admiring views of a dozen mountains and lakes. Wind-gnarled trees pose in occasional clusters. Scraggly, red-leaved dogbane plants dot the sand. At one point the trail splits, but the forks soon rejoin.

At the upper end of Moraine Lake's valley a side trail to the right dives down into the canyon. If you're taking the Moraine Lake loop, turn right and descend this steep, slippery trail. Use caution (and your hands) on the first, rugged 100-foot section of this path.

Moraine Lake's U-shaped valley was carved by the Lewis Glacier in the Ice Age. Leftover rock and sand were pushed to the glacier's toe as a moraine — the rounded ridge now cupping the lake. Later volcanic eruptions scattered pumice across the valley. Some of these floatable rocks are as big as basketballs.

To complete the Moraine Lake loop, hike to the far side of the lake and follow the trail up the ridge to the right. The climbers' trail back to Devils Lake is 0.8 mile beyond.

If you're climbing South Sister, however, go straight at the junction at the upper end of Moraine Lake's valley. The next 1.2 miles steepen drastically, finally leading to a resting point in a sandy saddle — the current terminal moraine of Lewis Glacier, overlooking a small green cirque lake. A climbers' trail from Green Lakes joins here on the right. The route to the summit heads up the ridge to the left. After 0.7 mile, crest the lip of South Sister's broad crater. Follow the rim to the right 0.4 mile to the summit, a rocky ridgecrest with a benchmark but no climbers' register. Bend, Sisters, and Redmond are clearly visible in the Central Oregon flatlands. To the north, the green Chambers Lakes dot the barren, glacial landscape below Middle Sister.

Moraine Lake and Broken Top from the loop.   *Opposite: Teardrop Pool atop South Sister.*

56   Sisters Mirror Lake

Moderate (to Sisters Mirror Lake)
8 miles round-trip
700 feet elevation gain
Open mid-July through October
Map: Three Sisters Wilderness (USFS)

Moderate (to Le Conte Crater)
7 miles round-trip
1000 feet elevation gain

Here's a hike with 2 very different options. If you enjoy exploring alpine lakes, the heather meadows around Sisters Mirror Lake are ideal. If you're in the mood for a volcanic viewpoint instead, choose the other fork of this trail and climb to Le Conte Crater, a miniature cinder cone wedged between Wickiup Plain and South Sister's rugged Rock Mesa lava flow. If you can't decide, why not do both? The combined loop is still only a moderate, 10.4-mile hike.

Start by driving 27 miles west of Bend on the Cascade Lakes Highway. Beyond the Mt. Bachelor Ski Area 6.5 miles, turn left at Devils Lake Campground. Park on the left of the campground loop at the sign for the Elk-Devils Lake Trail.

The trail promptly passes under the highway through a large culvert. After half a mile the path joins an abandoned, dusty road. This cat track was one of several bulldozed by a California mining company to reach claims staked before the Wilderness Act banned new claims. The company's threat to strip-mine Rock Mesa's pumice for cat litter ended with a $2 million buyout by Congress in 1983.

After half a mile on the road, turn right onto a heavily used but poorly marked side trail. Follow this path uphill for 1 mile to a trail junction at the edge of Wickiup Plain, a plateau of pumice and bunchgrass with a dramatic view of South Sister. If you're only going to Le Conte Crater, go straight here and head for the little cinder cone at the far upper end of the prairie. But to see Sisters Mirror Lake, turn left.

If you head left toward the lake, keep left at all junctions for another 1.4 miles to the Pacific Crest Trail. Then turn left on the PCT for 0.6 mile. The lake is too shallow for swimming and doesn't reflect South Sister very well, since only the tip of the peak is visible. But no matter; the alpine ambience here is the main attraction. Sit on the rocks at the far end of the lake to admire the natural rock garden of heather. If you have a compass and some pathfinding skills, try prowling cross-country to find a few of the 2 dozen ponds clustered within the square mile to the west.

Backpackers must bring a permit and should take care to camp in forest — not on the fragile meadow plants. Campfires are banned within 100 feet of any lake or trail.

To visit Le Conte Crater on the return trip, hike back on the PCT, following it 2.2 miles as it skirts House Rock and crosses a corner of Wickiup Plain. At a junction, turn right for 0.4 mile to the base of Le Conte Crater, a little, round-

South Sister from Wickiup Plain.   Opposite: Floating pumice in Sisters Mirror Lake.

topped cinder cone at the upper edge of WickiupPlain. From here climb cross-country up the meadowed slope to the crater rim. The crater bowl holds snow until mid-August. South Sister rises almost overhead. Rock Mesa is a sea of jumbled lava at your feet. To the southeast are Broken Top, Mt. Bachelor, and the lakes of the Cascade Lakes Highway.

Climb back down the cinder cone, turn left on the trail across Wickiup Plain, and follow signs for Devils Lake to return to the car.

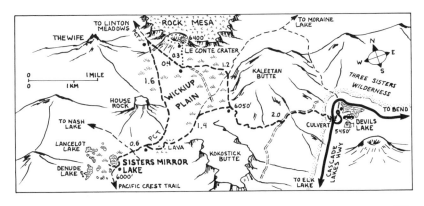

57 Horse Lake

Moderate
8.8-mile loop
600 feet elevation gain
Open late June through November
Map: Three Sisters Wilderness (USFS)

This popular loop heads deep into the rolling forests of the Three Sisters Wilderness. At Horse Lake, a fisherman's trail leads around the shore to a dramatic rock peninsula — the ideal spot for lunch. On the hike back, take a short, little-known side path to Colt Lake, a miniature version of Horse Lake. Mosquitoes are a problem throughout July.

Drive the Cascade Lakes Highway 31 miles west of Bend to Elk Lake, turn west at the sign for the Elk Lake Trailhead, and park at the turnaround. The trail forks after 50 yards — the start of the loop. Keep right, following the pointer for Horse Lake. This dusty, heavily used path climbs gradually 1.3 miles to a forested pass, crosses the Pacific Crest Trail, and then gradually descends 2 miles to a 4-way trail junction in a meadow. You can't see Horse Lake from here, but if you take the faint, unsigned trail straight ahead 300 yards you'll find the shore.

From this perspective, Horse Lake is likely to be a disappointment. No trace remains of the shelter that once stood here. The beachless shore is densely forested and so heavily trammeled that areas have been closed for restoration. So continue to the right on an unmaintained path around the lake to the much nicer far shore. Tennis shoes may get wet on this route, for some areas are a little boggy. Also expect to step over a few small logs along the way.

The less-visited, far shore of the lake has a view of Mt. Bachelor and a cinder cone named Red Top. Explore the long, blocky rock peninsula that juts far into

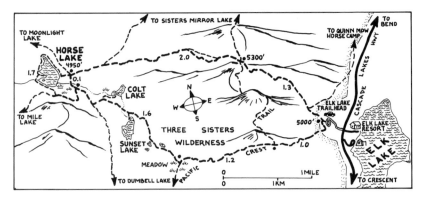

Island behind Horse Lake's peninsula.   Opposite: Gray jay ("camp robber").

the lake, with deep water below cliffs on the left and a forested island on the right.

The peninsula itself is off-limits for camping. Campfires are banned within 100 feet of water or trails. Backpackers should bring a permit.

Just beyond the peninsula the path crosses the lake's gurgling outlet creek on stepping stones. After another 0.3 mile the shoreline path joins the well-maintained trail from Mile Lake. Turn left here, skirt some lovely meadows, and reach another trail junction in the woods. Turn right toward Dumbbell Lake. But at the next trail junction, 0.3 mile up this path, *do not* follow the "Dumbbell Lake" pointer. Instead go straight toward Sunset Lake.

The side trail to Colt Lake is not marked, so watch for it carefully. Just 170 steps beyond the trail junction with the "Sunset Lake" arrow, notice a faint path splitting off across a small meadow to the left. Follow this path 0.1 mile to the pretty lake, ringed with small meadow openings.

Continuing the loop on the main trail, notice Sunset Lake through the trees on the right. Nearly a mile later, the path joins the Pacific Crest Trail in an unnamed meadow. Turn left on the PCT for 1.2 miles and then follow signs to the Elk Lake Trailhead.

58   Doris and Cliff Lakes

Easy (to Doris Lake)
2.8 miles round-trip
400 feet elevation gain
Open late June through October
Map: Three Sisters Wilderness (USFS)

Difficult (to Cliff Lake Shelter)
14.8 miles round-trip
1600 feet elevation gain

The Six Lakes Trailhead near Elk Lake is the gateway to far more lakes than merely 6. The rolling forests in this portion of the Three Sisters Wilderness are polka-dotted with blue. An easy walk up this trail reaches the first 2 large lakes, with small beaches suitable for children. For a longer hike, continue to the picturesque shelter at Cliff Lake. Backpackers can explore even further through these lake-dotted forests to Mink Lake. Expect mosquitoes throughout July.

Start by driving 33.5 miles west of Bend on the Cascade Lakes Highway. Past the Elk Lake Resort 2.5 miles, turn right at the "Six Lakes Trailhead" sign and park at the end of the turnaround.

The trail climbs very gradually through a dry forest of lodgepole pine, twice crossing footbridges over the (usually dry) outlet creek of Blow Lake. After the second bridge, short side trails lead to the right to Blow Lake's narrow gravel beach. The main trail continues around the lake to its inlet and then follows this creek more than a mile to Doris Lake. Once again, watch for side paths leading to the shore, with its view of a small rocky butte. A peninsula of the lakeshore has been closed for restoration, but other picnic spots abound.

If you're heading on to Cliff Lake, continue nearly a mile on the main trail to a junction for Senoj Lake. Yes, this is "Jones" spelled backwards. Turn right, following the "PCT" arrow. The trail now switchbacks up a ridge into a cooler

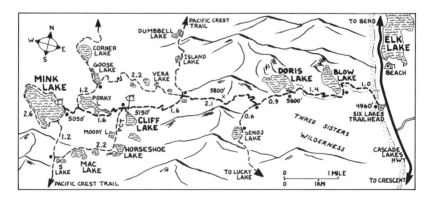

mountain hemlock forest with blue huckleberry bushes. Cross a pass and descend gradually to a junction with the Pacific Crest Trail. Turn left on the PCT for 1.6 miles, past small meadows and rock outcroppings.

The unmarked side trail to Cliff Lake is easy to miss. The trick is to watch for the well-marked trail junction to Porky Lake, beside a large rockslide. Stop here and backtrack 20 paces on the PCT. The path to Cliff Lake takes off here, skirting the base of the rockslide 150 yards to the hidden lake, backed by 50-foot cliffs. Flat, shaley rocks from the cliffs provide the foundation — and even some novel furniture — for the 3-sided shelter here.

Backpackers must bring permits and cannot use campfires within 100 feet of lakes or trails.

Other Hiking Options

The 18-mile round-trip hike to Mink Lake will interest backpackers, though the leaky shelter at this large, forest-rimmed lake provides little refuge. A tempting, slightly longer option is to return from Mink Lake on one of the trail loops exploring the countless smaller lakes in this area — either via Mac Lake or Goose Lake.

Doris Lake.   Opposite: Cliff Lake Shelter.

59 Muskrat Lake Shelter

Moderate
10 miles round-trip
200 feet elevation gain
Open mid-June to early November
Map: Three Sisters Wilderness (USFS)

This remarkably level hike follows the shore of Cultus Lake several miles, and then strikes off through the forest to a rustic log cabin by a pastoral lilypad lake.

To find the trailhead, drive the Cascade Lakes Highway 44 miles west of Bend to the sign for Cultus Lake Resort. Turn right onto paved Road 4635 for 1.8 miles, fork right toward the campground, and then keep to the right on a gravel road marked "Dead End." Half a mile further, after the road turns to a dirt track, the trailhead sign is on the left.

The trail joins a lakeshore path from the campground after 200 yards and proceeds around Cultus Lake to the right, offering views across the water to Cultus Mountain, a forested cinder cone. The mixed lodgepole pine and fir forests along the trail host woodland blooms: twinflower, prince's pine, and star-flowered smilacina.

The word *cultus* is a Chinook jargon term, used by Northwest Indians to describe wicked spirits and worthless places. Today the value of this clear, 3-mile-long lake is diminished only by the buzz of mosquitoes in July and the buzz of speedboats in August.

After 0.8 mile pass a long, sandy, swimmable beach. The semi-developed campsites here are popular with boaters. A mile beyond, leave the lakeshore at a broad bay. Ignore a side trail that joins from Corral Lakes, but turn right at the

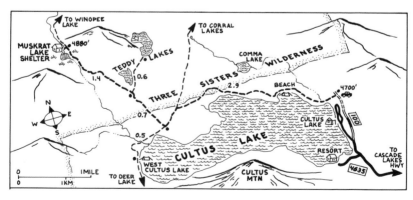

Muskrat Lake Shelter, an old trapper's cabin.   Opposite: Reeds in the lake.

second trail junction, following the "Winopee Lake" sign. This nearly level route passes a Wilderness boundary sign and a side trail for the Teddy Lakes before finally reaching a meadow-banked creek and Muskrat Lake.

The shelter here, though not shown on most Forest Service maps, is a spacious 15-by-25-foot log cabin, complete with wooden floor, 2 stoves, cupboards, folding chairs, and a sleeping loft. It is unlocked and open to the public. A path out the back door leads across a meadow to the lake. Aster, larkspur, and Indian paintbrush bloom in the meadow. Reeds and lilypads line the lake.

If you are backpacking do not depend on the shelter being unoccupied. As elsewhere in the Three Sisters Wilderness, remember to bring a permit and avoid tenting within 100 feet of any water source or trail.

Other Hiking Options
For a side trip, continue 0.3 mile around Cultus Lake to the lake's inlet creek. If the bridge which collapsed here in 1988 has been replaced, continue another 0.2 mile to West Cultus Lake Campground, not accessible by car.

A second side trip follows an 0.6-mile trail past the smaller Teddy Lake to the forested shore of the larger Teddy Lake.

McKenzie
Foothills

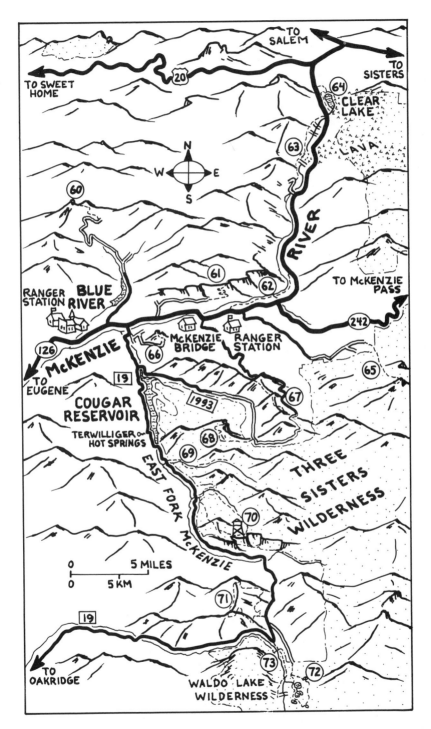

Opposite: French Pete Creek (Hike #69).

60 Tidbits Mountain

Easy
4 miles round-trip
1100 feet elevation gain
Open mid-June through October
Map: Tidbits Mtn. (USGS)

This little-known mountain near Blue River is a delightful tidbit for hikers. The pinnacled summit, where a lookout tower once stood, offers sweeping views from the Three Sisters to the Willamette Valley. The trail to the top traverses an old-growth forest of 6-foot-thick giants. Rhododendrons, gentians, and trilliums brighten the way. And although the path gains more than 1000 feet, the grade is gradual enough for children.

Drive 3 miles east of Blue River on Highway 126 and turn left onto Road 15 at the sign for Blue River Reservoir. Follow this road 4.8 miles to the end of the pavement, and then go straight on gravel Road 1509 for 8.3 winding miles. Half a mile past a green water tank turn left at a ridge-end and take the very steep Road 877 up the ridge 0.2 mile to a short spur on the left with a rough parking area.

The trail begins at the end of the parking area amid rhododendrons and beargrass, but soon dives into a forest of huge, ancient Douglas firs. Watch for wild ginger, vanilla leaf, and star-flowered smilacina.

After 1.3 miles reach a saddle with a trail junction and the collapsed remains of a 1930s-style Forest Service shelter. Turn left. The path soon traverses a large rockslide with impressive views over crumpled foothills to the northwest. Above the path are cliffs with interesting pinnacles — the finger-like "tidbits"

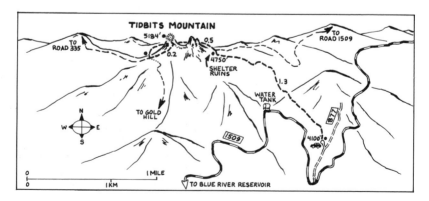

that give this mountain its name. In the middle of the slope ignore a side path switchbacking up to the left; this is an alternate return route from the summit. Continue straight, past scattered boards from the fallen lookout tower and huge bouquets of blue, cup-shaped gentian.

When the trail reaches a junction at a ridgecrest, switchback to the left on a path climbing the ridge. The forest dwindles here to wind-swept bonsai trees in a rock garden of yellow stonecrop and pink penstemon. Remains of a staircase reveal how the lookouts climbed the final 30 feet, but it's not difficult to scramble up the bare rock.

From the top you can survey the entire route of the hike and even spot your car. To the east are Cascade snowpeaks from Mt. Hood to Diamond Peak, with Black Butte and Mt. Bachelor peeking out from Central Oregon. To the west, look down the South Santiam, Calapooia, and McKenzie River valleys to the distant haze of the Willamette Valley.

To try the alternate route back from the summit, hike 50 yards down the main trail and turn left. This fainter path switchbacks through a high saddle before rejoining the main trail in 0.2 mile.

View from Tidbits Mountain.   *Opposite: Vanilla leaf.*

The Three Sisters from Frissell Trail.   Opposite: Chinkapin fruit ("porcupine egg").

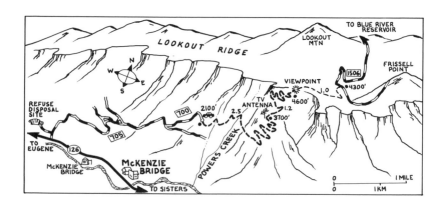

61   Frissell Trail

Difficult
7.4 miles round-trip
2500 feet elevation gain
Open May through November
Map: McKenzie Br. (USGS)

Conveniently near McKenzie Bridge, this challenging viewpoint hike provides a good dose of exercise. The trail switchbacks 15 times up the side of the McKenzie River canyon, emerging from the forest at an overlook of the Three Sisters and the McKenzie River Valley. The trail commemorates George Frissell, who in 1885 built the Log Cabin Inn, an historic stage stop still operating as a restaurant in McKenzie Bridge.

Turn off Highway 126 at a "Refuse Disposal Site" sign 1.2 miles west of McKenzie Bridge (or 8.1 miles east of Blue River). Follow gravel Road 705, keeping to the right at all junctions for 2.2 miles, and then fork left onto Road 700 for 0.7 mile to the unmarked trailhead at road's end. The parking area is very small.

The path sets off through a soothingly quiet Douglas fir forest with sword fern, Oregon grape, and salal. At 0.2, 0.5, and 0.6 mile the trail dips into ravines cut by small branches of Powers Creek. By the first switchback, at the 1.2-mile mark, the forest has changed to a drier mix of chinkapin, hazelnut, and some fir. This area is regrowing from a 1960s forest fire. By late summer, bracken fern can crowd the tread.

At 2.5 miles the first set of switchbacks ends on a knoll with a small cable television relay antenna and a glimpse across the McKenzie Valley to Castle Rock (Hike #66). For a more satisfying view, continue 1.2 miles uphill. Here the trail crosses a steep, open slope with yarrow, goldenrod, and scrub oak. Far below are a state airstrip and a tiny curve of the McKenzie River's whitewater. The Three Sisters rise ahead, with Mt. Bachelor to the right and Ollalie Ridge (Hike #67) among the green hills across the valley.

Though the Frissell Trail continues downhill a mile to Road 1506, this stretch is anticlimactic. Make the viewpoint your goal.

Other Hiking Options

The whole point of the Frissell Trail is exercise, but if you'd like a much smaller dose, start at the upper trailhead on Road 1506. To find it, drive 3 miles east of Blue River on Highway 126, turn onto Road 15 at the sign for Blue River Reservoir for 3.6 miles, and then take Road 1506 to the right for 11 miles. After a hairpin curve — and 0.3 mile before the road finally reaches a ridgecrest — watch for the trail on the right. The viewpoint is only 1 mile away and 300 feet uphill.

62 Lower McKenzie River Trail

Easy
7.8 miles round-trip
200 feet elevation gain
Open except in winter storms
Map: Belknap Spr. (USGS)

Ancient Douglas fir and red cedar 6 feet in diameter tower above the McKenzie's roaring whitewater along this easily accessible trail. The hike ambles to Belknap Hot Springs, an old-time, woodsy resort with a tempting 102-degree swimming pool. Hikers with 2 cars can spare themselves the return walk by arranging a shuttle. Hikers with no car at all can still join this hike by taking the Eugene city bus to the trailhead.

This is a nice hike to repeat in different seasons. Snow seldom closes this portion of the McKenzie River Trail. By April, dogwood trees fill the understory with their white crosses, and trilliums dot the forest floor. In late May, crowds of fishermen arrive, but so do delicate pink deer-head orchids and great yellow bunches of Oregon grape blooms. And in fall, chanterelle mushrooms sprout in the forest while vine maple turns the river banks scarlet.

Start at the McKenzie Ranger Station parking lot 2.5 miles east of McKenzie Bridge on Highway 126. (The bus to this point leaves the Eugene downtown transit station Monday through Saturday at 8:22am. The return trip leaves the ranger station weekdays at 4:03pm and 7:23pm, and Saturdays at 5:53pm. Round-trip fare is $1.30 weekdays and 60 cents on Saturday. Fares and schedules may change; check by calling 687-5555.)

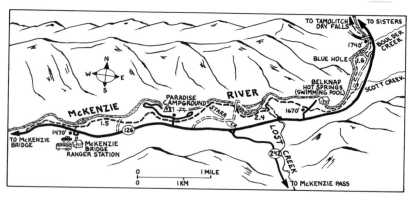

Old-growth Douglas fir along trail.   Opposite: Dogwood.

Cross the highway from the parking lot's west entrance and enter the forest on an obvious but unsigned trail. After 50 yards, reach the riverbank and turn right on the McKenzie River Trail through a lovely old-growth forest. At the 0.7-mile mark the trail detours inland for 1.5 miles to avoid riverfront summer cabins and Paradise Campground. Some highway noise is audible along this section. Back in the solitude of the riverbank, the trail crosses rushing, 40-foot-wide Lost Creek on a footbridge at a nice picnic spot.

Finally the trail winds away from the river again and comes to a paved road with a double yellow center line. If you wish to melt off trail dust in Belknap Hot Springs' steamy pool, walk left down this road 0.2 mile and sign in at the lodge. The pool overlooking the river is open 365 days a year 9am to 9pm, and the fee is a mere $2. Bring a suit, as cutoffs are not allowed. Simon Belknap, who staked a claim to the springs in 1870, claimed the waters cured "female weakness, inflammations both external and internal, and general debility." Perhaps so.

Other Hiking Options

The McKenzie River Trail continues 21.6 miles past the Belknap Hot Springs road — all the way to the McKenzie's headwaters. Upper portions of this trail are described in hikes #63 Tamolitch Dry Falls and #64 Clear Lake Loop.

63   Tamolitch Dry Falls

Easy (to Tamolitch Falls)
4.2 miles round-trip
200 feet elevation gain
Open mid-April to mid-December
Maps: Tamolitch Falls, Clear L. (USGS)

Moderate (to Hwy. 126, with shuttle)
7.5 miles one-way
800 feet elevation gain
Open May to mid-November

The entire McKenzie River vanishes into the ground along this scenic and remote portion of the McKenzie River Trail. After an eerie phantom "waterfall" and a stunning turquoise pool, the river splashes once again through mossy old-growth forests.

Hikers with children can turn back after ambling upriver to the dry falls. Others will want to continue on to reliably wet Koosah Falls and Sahalie Falls. The longer hike requires a shuttle vehicle — perhaps a bicycle stashed in anticipation of the easy downhill ride back to the lower trailhead.

To reach the lower trailhead, drive Highway 126 to the upper end of Trailbridge Reservoir (14 miles east of McKenzie Bridge), turn left at the "EWEB Powerhouse" sign, cross a bridge, and turn right. At a curve 0.4 mile up this gravel road, park by a hiker-symbol sign on the right. (To leave a shuttle at the upper trailhead, drive 6.6 miles past Trailbridge Reservoir — 0.6 mile beyond the Sahalie Falls turnoff — to a small pullout on the left where the highway crosses the McKenzie River.)

The first 1.1 mile of the hike is nearly level, through an old-growth forest of Douglas fir and droopy red cedar beside the rushing river. Then the trail climbs gradually through a moss-covered lava flow to an overlook of deep blue-green Tamolitch Pool, whose only apparent inlet is a dry waterfall, yet from which the McKenzie River mysteriously emerges. In Chinook jargon, the trade language

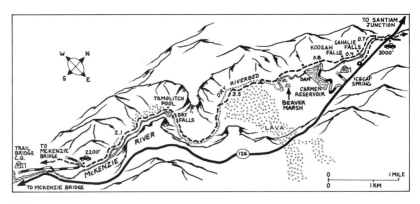

of Northwest Indians, *tamolitch* means "bucket," and the name fits this cliff-rimmed basin. Lava flows buried the riverbed above here 1500 years ago, but the river percolates through the porous rock to underwater springs in Tamolitch Pool.

Those continuing past Tamolitch Dry Falls now enter the quietest section of the entire 26.5-mile McKenzie River Trail — a riverless canyon floor inhabited by huge mossy maples and silent Douglas fir. After 3 miles pass Beaver Marsh, where the McKenzie traditionally seeped into the ground, and in another 0.5 mile reach Carmen Reservoir's dam, where the river currently disappears. The Eugene Water and Electric Board diverts most of the river through a 2-mile tunnel to Smith Reservoir, where a second tunnel drops it to the Trailbridge power plant.

The McKenzie is in full force, however, at 70-foot Koosah Falls and 100-foot Sahalie Falls. These falls are even more spectacular from the trail's side of the river than from the highway's side, where the Forest Service has built massive concrete viewpoints.

Tamolitch Pool.   Opposite: Trillium.

64 Clear Lake

Easy
7-mile loop
200 feet elevation gain
Open May to mid-November
Maps: Clear L., Santiam Jct., Echo Mtn.
(USGS)

Three thousand years ago lava flows from the High Cascades dammed the McKenzie River, creating a lake so clear, cold, and calm that ghostly tree snags are still visible under its 100-foot-deep waters. The stroll around Clear Lake offers lots of variety: huge springs, lava crossings, old-growth forests — even a resort with a good fifty-cent cup of coffee.

Drive Highway 126 to the massive sign announcing the upper end of the McKenzie River Trail (2 miles south of the Highway 20 junction or 1.8 miles north of the Clear Lake Recreation Area turnoff). Take the rutted side road 100 yards and park near a footbridge. The trail starts out along Fish Lake Creek — a rushing stream from March to May when the lake at its source brims with snowmelt. But the creek is dry the rest of the year when Fish Lake is a meadow. The trail soon crosses a gravel road and enters an old-growth forest of massive Douglas firs, with an understory of delicate vanilla-leaf and scraggly yew trees.

After 1 mile join the footpath around Clear Lake and go left across a footbridge. Soon there's a view across the lake to the resort. This portion of Clear Lake has the ancient underwater snags, though they're more impressive from a boat. Next the trail detours around a rushing, 300-foot-long river that emerges from a dry lava landscape at Great Springs' astonishing pool. Though chilly, the springs' constant 38-degree Fahrenheit temperature keeps Clear Lake from freezing in winter.

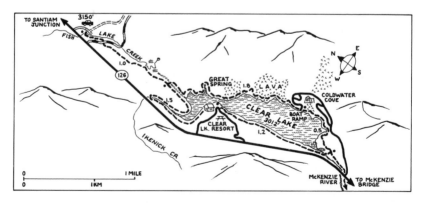

Paved trail through lava at Clear Lake.   Opposite: Footbridge over outlet river.

On either side of the Coldwater Cove boat ramp — where golden-mantled ground squirrels are so bold they sit on picnickers' laps — the trail has been paved to simplify the crossing of rough lava flows. Half a mile beyond the boat ramp, turn right on a fork marked "Clear Lake Trail" and 200 yards later cross a footbridge over the lake's glassy outlet, the beginning of the McKenzie River. After another mile along the lakeshore, with some traffic noise audible, come to a picnic area and the small resort, offering groceries, rowboat rentals, and a cafe. Walk past a dozen rental cabins to the resumption of the lakeshore trail. The path follows a narrow arm of Clear Lake, crosses Ikenick Creek near the highway, climbs over a peninsula of the lake, and rejoins the McKenzie River Trail 1 mile from the hike's start.

Other Hiking Options
   To reduce the hike from 7 to 5 miles — an easier distance for children — start your walk around the lake at the Clear Lake Resort.

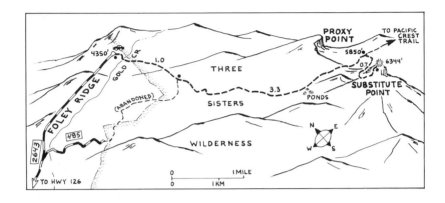

65   Substitute Point

Moderate
10 miles round-trip
2000 feet elevation gain
Open July through October
Map: Three Sisters Wilderness (USFS)

This rocky knob, rising from the forest 6 miles due west of the Three Sisters, is a balcony seat for the snowy triplets' big panorama. The view seems even more impressive because the trail here offers no views along the way, climbing gradually through a dense forest of mountain hemlock.

Substitute Point and nearby Proxy Point were named by a 1916 survey party as 2 possible locations for a triangulation station. Substitute Point won both the station and a later fire lookout tower. The tower is gone, but the summit stone still bears the carefully engraved names of lookouts from the 1930s and 40s.

Turn off Highway 126 half a mile east of the McKenzie Bridge Ranger Station and follow Foley Ridge Road 2643 uphill for 7.6 paved miles and another 3.7 miles of gravel to the Foley Ridge Trailhead at road's end. Expect a few horse trailers here; this trail is chiefly used by equestrians heading to the Pacific Crest Trail at Linton Meadows.

The path descends briefly to Gold Creek and then begins a long, steady uphill grade, climbing so gradually the 2000 feet of elevation gain are not arduous. Rhododendrons bloom throughout these forests in early July. Coolwort and bunchberry provide white flowers in late summer.

At 3.2 miles notice a dragonfly pond among the trees to the right. The trail crests at a saddle 0.6 mile beyond, then crosses a rockslide, circumvents a patch

South Sister from Substitute Point.   Opposite: Carved names of lookouts at summit.

of blowdown from a 1990 storm, and reaches a junction. Turn right on the trail winding up through the forest 0.7 mile to Substitute Point's summit.

South Sister is impressively close, while North and Middle Sister are partly blocked by The Husband's orange crags. To the right, notice Mt. Bachelor and The Wife above Rock Mesa's barren lava flow. Other summits are visible from Mt. Jefferson to Diamond Peak. The only lake in sight is Kidney Lake, in line with Sphinx Butte.

66 Castle Rock

Easy
2 miles round-trip
600 feet elevation gain
Open April to mid-December
Map: McKenzie Br. (USGS)

Viewpoint climbs don't come much easier than this. After a scant mile of well-graded switchbacks through the forest, this path leads to a cliff-edge lookout site overlooking the McKenzie River Valley from Blue River to the Three Sisters.

Drive Highway 126 to the turnoff for Cougar Reservoir (4.4 miles east of Blue River or 4.8 miles west of McKenzie Bridge). Follow Road 19 for half a mile, continue straight on paved Road 410 toward the Cougar Dam powerhouse for 0.4 mile, turn left onto gravel Road 2639 for half a mile, and then turn right onto Road 480. Follow this one-lane gravel road uphill 5.8 miles to its end at a very small parking area.

After a few yards the trail forks; head uphill to the right. The Douglas fir forest here is so dense that only the most shade-tolerant vanilla leaf, vine maple, and Oregon grape can grow beneath it. After climbing steadily 0.8 mile, pass beneath some cliffs and enter a steep, dry meadow dotted with manzanita bushes, chinkapin trees, and gnarled black oaks. At a saddle, follow the bare ridge to the summit on the left.

From the old lookout site, the long trough of the McKenzie River Valley is very clearly U-shaped in cross section — evidence the canyon was widened by Ice Age glaciers spilling down from the Three Sisters. Note the green links of Tokatee Golf Course far below and a scrap of Cougar Reservoir to the south. To the east

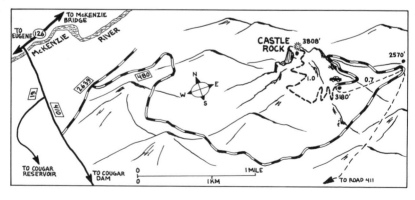

Madrone atop Castle Rock.   Opposite: Oregon grape leaf.

are Mt. Washington and the Three Sisters, while the horizon in all other directions teems with the jumbled ridges of the Old Cascades, patchworked with clearcuts.

Other Hiking Options

If this hike's too short, or if you want to avoid driving the final, rough 2 miles of Road 480, park at the lower Castle Rock Trailhead. Where Road 480 makes a hairpin curve at a saddle, look for the inconspicuous trail taking off uphill. From here it's 1.7 miles to the top, with 1238 feet elevation gain.

67   Olallie Ridge

Easy (to viewpoint)
6.4 miles round-trip
500 feet elevation gain
Open late June to early November
Map: Three Sisters Wilderness (USFS)

Not too many years ago this scenic ridge was part of the high country wildlands stretching from McKenzie Bridge to the Three Sisters. Construction of Road 1993 separated Olallie Ridge from the Wilderness with a moat of clearcuts, but the ridgecrest Olallie Trail is still intact — a relatively level, pleasantly wooded path to a viewpoint of the big, snowy mountains to the east.

The August huckleberries that once attracted Indians to this ridge are still here, too. In fact, *olallie* is a Chinook jargon word meaning "berry." Early forest rangers prized the ridge's meadows as a refueling stop for their mounts. Rangers named Horsepasture Mountain and built a (now vanished) shelter at Horsepasture Saddle. In the 1930s and 40s, a heavy-gauge telephone wire connected fire lookout towers atop Horsepasture Mountain and Lamb Butte with the ranger station in McKenzie Bridge. O-shaped ceramic insulators from the old telephone line are still visible on trailside trees.

Start by driving Highway 126 to McKenzie Bridge. At the east end of the river bridge, turn south onto paved Horse Creek Road for 1.7 miles. Just after the Horse Creek Group Campground turn right onto Road 1993 and follow this one-lane paved route for 8.6 winding, uphill miles and park at the second hiker-symbol sign on the right. (Ignore the first sign for the Olallie Trail alongside Road 1993; this lower portion of the trail is very steep.)

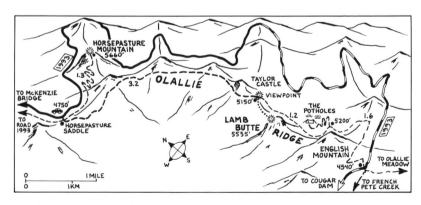

The trail begins amid a patch of coneflowers — odd brown blooms in the sunflower family, but lacking petals. After just 80 yards, reach a 4-way trail junction at Horsepasture Saddle. Continue straight, contouring along a wooded slope full of flowers: Washington lilies, thimbleberry, star-flowered smilacina, and prince's pine.

After 2.6 miles the trail heads uphill, traversing the west side of Taylors Castle. Then the trail crosses a saddle to the east side of the ridge and suddenly emerges from the woods, eyeball to eyeball with the Three Sisters. Mt. Bachelor and the broken tip of Broken Top peer out from Central Oregon. The sides of the trail here are thick with huckleberry bushes and wildflowers, providing a pleasant turnaround point.

Other Hiking Options

If you have a bit more energy — or an extra car — there are three tempting choices. First, you could climb Horsepasture Mountain to the superior viewpoint there. A sign at Horsepasture Saddle directs you up a faint, switchbacking trail 1.3 miles to the former lookout site. Second, you could bushwhack to the scenic summit of Lamb Butte. Only adventurers with pathfinding skills should attempt this 0.6-mile climb, leaving the Olallie Trail at the saddle near the viewpoint and following the trailless ridge south. Finally, if you have a second car, you could shuttle it to the trailhead beside English Mountain (11.1 miles further along Road 1993) and then hike one-way for 6 miles along Olallie Ridge. Backpackers on this route will find a campsite at the Potholes, a boggy meadow down a 0.6-mile side trail.

Old-growth along Olallie Trail.   Opposite: Insulator from old lookout phone line.

68   Lowder Mountain

Easy
5.6 miles round-trip
900 feet elevation gain
Open late June through October
Map: Three Sisters Wilderness (USFS)

At first the summit of flat-topped Lowder Mountain appears to be nothing more than a forest-rimmed meadow. Only when you venture to the wind-bent trees on its eastern side do you discover the mountain's monumental cliffs. Two lakes shimmer nearly 1000 feet below. And beyond, the Three Sisters loom like great white ghosts.

Drive Highway 126 to the turnoff for Cougar Reservoir (4.4 miles east of Blue River or 4.8 miles west of McKenzie Bridge). Take Road 19 half a mile to a junction, turn right, and follow Road 19 another 2.5 miles to the reservoir. Turn left across the dam on Road 1993. Follow this road first on pavement, then on gravel, for a total of 11.1 miles uphill to a junction at a pass. Park at a hiker-symbol sign here.

Start out on the uphill trail signed for Lowder Mountain. The well-graded path switchbacks a few times in an old-growth Douglas fir forest, then levels off and traverses three sloping meadows. The openings offer views across French Pete Creek's valley (Hike #69) to Olallie Mountain and snowy Mt. Bachelor. Thimbleberry and bracken fern are mixed with coneflower, an oddly unpetaled sunflower relative.

At the 2-mile mark, turn right at a trail junction in another meadow and begin switchbacking steeply uphill. After nearly half a mile of this effort you suddenly reach Lowder Mountain's barren summit plain. The trail's tread is obscure here,

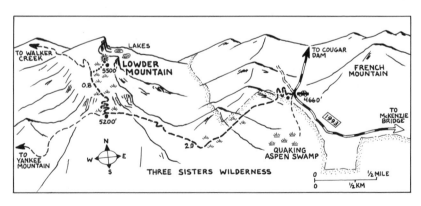

Two lakes below Lowder Mountain's cliffs.   Opposite: Coneflower.

but rock cairns mark the route 0.2 mile across the plain, past clumps of trees. Just before the trail reenters the forest to begin its descent toward Walker Creek, leave the trail and walk up through the field to the right 0.2 mile to the hidden cliffs, and a breathtaking view of the High Cascades from Mt. Hood to the Three Sisters.

Other Hiking Options

Romantic souls sometimes camp atop Lowder Mountain to watch the Three Sisters burn red in the sunset. Tent sites abound, but bring a permit and any water you might need.

69   French Pete Creek

Easy (to bridgeless crossing)
6 miles round-trip
600 feet elevation gain
Open late March to mid-December
Map: Three Sisters Wilderness (USFS)

Moderate (to 5-mile marker)
10 miles round-trip
1000 feet elevation gain

French Pete Creek was the first low-elevation valley to be preserved because of the outcry over Oregon's vanishing old-growth forests. The original Three Sisters Wilderness included only feebly forested, high-elevation land. After 14 years of ardent protest by hikers, students, and environmentalists, French Pete was added in 1978.

This valley aroused such passion because of the sheer grandeur of the mossy jungle along its cascading mountain creek. Gargantuan Douglas firs and 1000-year-old cedars tower above a green carpet of sword ferns, twinflower, and Oregon grape. But the French Pete Trail's charming footbridges also won a number of converts. Old-growth logs, fitted with handrails, spanned a dozen side creeks and crossed the main stream 4 times.

Now all but one of these scenic bridges have rotted away. The Forest Service, reluctant to cut old-growth trees to replace the spans, surveyed a new trail route entirely on the creek's north bank. With trail funds low, the Forest Service is looking for volunteers to help finish the route. Until then, hikers will find this popular trail a bit rough, with a tricky bridgeless crossing at the 3-mile mark.

Drive Highway 126 to the turnoff for Cougar Reservoir (4.4 miles east of Blue River or 4.8 miles west of McKenzie Bridge). Take Road 19 half a mile to a junction, turn right, and follow Road 19 another 10 paved miles. A mile beyond the end of the reservoir turn left at a sign indicating the French Pete Trailhead.

The path climbs very gradually, at times through wooded benchlands out of sight of the creek. After 0.9 mile the path dips into a side canyon to cross 4-foot-wide Yankee Creek. Then, at the 1.7-mile mark, the trail crosses French Pete Creek on a huge old-growth log with a handrail. Eventually this old footbridge will be removed and the trail will continue along the creek's steep north slope. In the meantime, cross the 100-foot span and follow the trail on the south bank 1.3 miles to a bridgeless crossing of French Pete Creek. This makes a good turnaround point for hikers with children.

If you're continuing, cross the creek as cautiously as possible on the available wiggly logs and slippery rocks — or safer yet, bring old tennis shoes and wade. After the crossing, the French Pete Trail is less well maintained but far less crowded. Continue 1.8 pleasant miles until the trail crosses a large, bouldery side creek. Just beyond is a picnickable flat beside French Pete Creek. A ceramic "5" mile marker is 200 yards up the trail. This makes a good stopping point, for

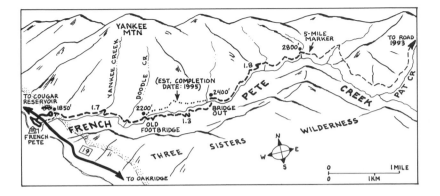

the path now begins a long traverse up the canyon slopes, leaving French Pete Creek for good.

Once very popular with backpackers, the French Pete Trail is now restricted by Wilderness rules banning campfires within 100 feet of water or trails — which affects virtually all flat ground in this narrow canyon. Permits are required.

Other Hiking Options

With a car shuttle, you can hike the 9.8-mile length of the French Pete Valley one-way — and all downhill. Leave a car at the trailhead described above and drive a second vehicle back to Cougar Dam. Cross the dam and follow Road 1993 for 15.4 miles to the upper Pat Saddle Trailhead beside English Mountain (see Hike #67).

Single-log footbridge.   Opposite: French Pete Creek.

Rebel Rock Lookout.   Below: Footbridge over Rebel Creek.

70   Rebel Creek

Easy (to second bridge)
2.2 miles round-trip
400 feet elevation gain
Open late March to mid-December
Map: Three Sisters Wilderness (USFS)

Difficult (to Rebel Rock lookout)
12.3-mile loop
3300 feet elevation gain
Open mid-June through October

The old-growth forests along this mountain stream are as grand as those along nearby French Pete Creek, but because this area is less well known, it's much less crowded. What's more, energetic hikers can continue up Rebel Creek on a challenging loop past a hidden lookout building to a viewpoint of the Three Sisters.

Start by driving Highway 126 to the turnoff for Cougar Reservoir (4.4 miles east of Blue River or 4.8 miles west of McKenzie Bridge). Take Road 19 half a mile to a junction, turn right, and follow Road 19 another 13 paved miles to Rebel Trailhead.

The trail begins at the message board and, after 100 yards, forks. Turn left on the Rebel Creek Trail, traversing a second-growth forest for half a mile. Then switchback down to cross the creek on a 100-foot bridge built of a single huge log. Here the trail enters a cathedral-like grove of ancient Douglas fir and drooping cedar, many 7 feet in diameter.

At the 1.1-mile mark cross the creek again on a smaller bridge. Hikers with children should declare victory here and turn back, for the trail beyond this point leaves the creek and climbs for 4.6 miles along a canyon slope. If you're intrigued by the hidden lookout tower, however, and prepared for an athletic loop hike, continue onward.

As the Rebel Creek Trail climbs, the forest changes to mountain hemlock, with an understory of rhododendron and bunchberry. After crossing a small branch of Rebel Creek and switchbacking up the head of the valley, turn right at a trail junction. This route soon traverses a large, steep meadow with waist-high bracken fern and thimbleberry. Look for purple aster and red paintbrush.

When the trail reenters the woods and reaches a windswept ridgecrest, be sure to look behind for the view of Rebel Rock's thumb-shaped rock pillar, for this is as close as the trail comes to that landmark.

Note that the Rebel Rock lookout tower is not on Rebel Rock, but rather on a cliff edge a mile to the west. And since the trail bypasses the tower in the woods, it's easy to miss. As you continue up the ridgecrest watch for 4 large rock cairns beside the trail. Turn left here on a faint trail 100 yards to the hidden lookout. No longer in use but well preserved, the squat, square building has a railed porch with a view across the South Fork McKenzie River Canyon to Chucksney Mountain (Hike #71). To the east is white-topped Mt. Bachelor.

An even better mountain view waits half a mile further along the loop trail, where the path crests a meadowed ridge. Here you can finally spot the Three Sisters and Mt. Jefferson.

After the viewpoint the trail dives down a large meadow. Bracken obscures the tread; watch for a switchback to the left 0.6 mile down and a switchback to the right 0.2 mile beyond. The path then reenters the forest for the long descent to the car.

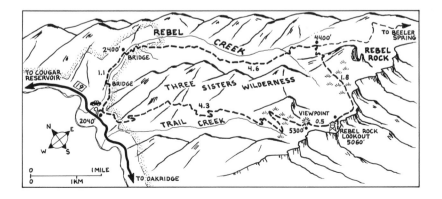

71   Chucksney Mountain

Difficult
10.3-mile loop
2000 feet elevation gain
Open late June through October
Map: Chucksney Mtn. (USGS)

This invigorating loop climbs along forested ridges to the crest of Chucksney Mountain, where it ambles more than a mile through delightful summit meadows with views of the Three Sisters. On the way down, the path visits a hidden glen — the headwaters of Box Canyon Creek.

To drive here from the McKenzie Highway, take the turnoff for Cougar Reservoir (4.4 miles east of Blue River or 4.8 miles west of McKenzie Bridge) and follow paved Road 19 for 25.5 miles to Box Canyon Campground. To drive here from Highway 58, take the Westfir exit near Oakridge and continue straight past Westfir's covered bridge onto Road 19. Follow this paved route for 31.4 miles to Box Canyon Campground. Opposite the campground entrance is the historic Box Canyon Guard Station, restored as an information center.

Trailhead parking is at the far right end of the campground. The Forest Service promotes the campground as an equestrian center, but horse use of the Chucksney Mountain trails is light.

Keep right at each of 3 trail junctions in the first 0.3 mile, ending up on the Chucksney Mountain Loop Trail #3306. This path climbs 2 long switchbacks before traversing north along a steep slope. At first the Douglas fir forest is greened with sword fern, Oregon grape, and star-flowered smilacina. Higher, the forest shifts to mountain hemlock with beargrass and vanilla leaf.

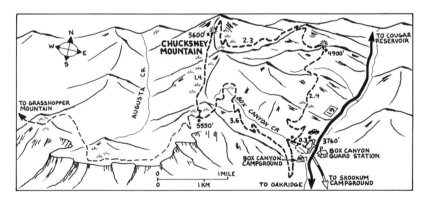

South Sister from Chucksney Mountain's summit ridge.   Opposite: Larkspur.

A bare, rocky ridge-end at the 2.7-mile mark provides a nice view across the forests to the Three Sisters and Mt. Washington. After another 0.6 mile of climbing to a ridgecrest, switchback briefly downhill and then contour around a large basin — an Ice Age cirque.

Finally the trail switchbacks up to the open crest of Chucksney Mountain's rocky summit ridge. To the east, the Three Sisters, Broken Top, and Mt. Bachelor rise above the chasm of the South Fork McKenzie River. To the west, Grasshopper Mountain and Hiyu Ridge battle an encroaching maze of logging roads.

The loop trail continues on the far side of the crest, heading south through the summit meadows. The route loses a few feet of elevation but then levels off for more than a mile. At the end of the summit ridge descend through a meadow with a glimpse of Diamond Peak and turn left on the Grasshopper Trail. The next mile of this path explores a high basin with scattered meadows. Look here for blue aster, pearly everlasting, purple larkspur, and petal-less, brown coneflower. Finally the path crosses (sometimes dry) Box Canyon Creek and launches downhill through the woods for the steep, 2.9-mile return to the campground.

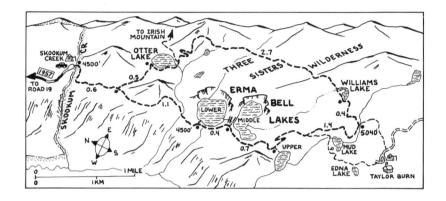

72   Erma Bell Lakes

Easy (to Middle Erma Bell Lake)
4.2 miles round-trip
300 feet elevation gain
Open mid-June to mid-November
Map: Three Sisters Wilderness (USFS)

Moderate (to Williams Lake)
8.4-mile loop
800 feet elevation gain

Lower and Middle Erma Bell Lakes, separated by a small waterfall, are among the most heavily visited destinations in the high country forests north of Waldo Lake — perhaps because the trail here is so delightfully level that even small children can manage the hike.

To be sure, popularity has brought some restrictions. Portions of the lakes' shores are roped off for restoration. Within 250 feet of any of the 3 Erma Bell Lakes or Otter Lake, camping is only allowed at approved sites marked by a post. Permits are required. But it's not too hard to outdistance the crowds here. Simply continue on a longer loop to Williams Lake, and pick up 2 other lakes in the bargain.

From the McKenzie Highway, take the turnoff for Cougar Reservoir (4.4 miles east of Blue River or 4.8 miles west of McKenzie Bridge) and follow paved Road 19 for 25.6 miles. Just after the Box Canyon Guard Station, turn left on gravel Road 1957 for 3.6 miles to Skookum Campground. To drive here from the Willamette Highway, take the Westfir exit near Oakridge and continue straight past Westfir's covered bridge onto Road 19. Follow this paved route for 31.3 miles to a pass just before the historic Box Canyon Guard Station and turn right on gravel Road 1957 to its end at Skookum Campground.

Middle Erma Bell Lake.   Opposite: Queen's cup.

From the campground parking lot, the trail crosses a creek on a large footbridge. The name Skookum is appropriate for this rushing stream; in Chinook jargon the word means "powerful." The Erma Bell Lakes, on the other hand, are named for a Forest Service bookkeeper who died in an automobile accident in Troutdale in 1918. Alongside the broad trail, look for rhododendrons and trilliums blooming in June. Other woodland flowers bloom here in July: bunchberry, star-flowered smilacina, and vanilla leaf.

After 0.6 mile go straight at a trail junction, and in another 1.1 mile reach a "No Camping" sign. A short side trail to the left leads to deep, blue Lower Erma Bell Lake. None of the lakes on this hike has a mountain view or an established trail around its lakeshore.

Continue 0.4 mile up the main trail to Middle Erma Bell Lake. Just above the waterfall, take a side trail left across the outlet creek to find a pleasant stretch of shore where children can dabble sticks in the water and watch dragonflies.

To continue the loop on the main trail, hike past Upper Erma Bell Lake to a trail junction. Keep left on the Erma Bell Trail for 1.4 miles to another trail junction just before a footbridge. Don't cross the bridge; turn left, and in 0.4 mile reach Williams Lake.

Williams Lake's bedrock shore was scraped smooth by glaciers during the Ice Age and even shows scratches left by rocks dragged beneath the ice. This entire area is still recovering from glaciation that ended just 6000 years ago. Humps of bare rock protrude here and there from soils so thin only lodgepole pine and beargrass survive.

Beyond Williams Lake the trail gradually descends 2.4 miles to the Irish Mountain Trail junction; turn left and pass Otter Lake to complete the loop.

73 North Fork Middle Fork

Easy (to river crossing)
6 miles round-trip
100 feet elevation gain
Open mid-April to mid-December
Map: Waldo Lake Wilderness (USFS)

Moderate (to waterfall)
8.6 miles round-trip
500 feet elevation gain

This remarkably level trail through a lovely old-growth grove leads to a crossing of the Willamette River's wildest branch: the North Fork Middle Fork, untamed outlet of Waldo Lake. If you're adventurous enough to cross the river on fallen logs, you can continue to an overlook of a roaring waterfall.

To drive here from Highway 58, take the Westfir exit near Oakridge and continue straight past Westfir's covered bridge onto Road 19. Follow this paved route for 29.4 miles to a hiker-symbol sign on a tight curve just before the road begins climbing to a pass. Pull into a parking area on the right.

The trail sets off through a classic old-growth forest — a sheltered, well-watered valley where hemlock, fir, and cedar grow over 200 feet tall. Appropriately, not all the trunks are 7 feet in diameter. As part of the cycle some older trees have fallen, providing light and soil for saplings and a lush, green understory of moss, vine maple, sword fern. There's also a host of white wildflowers: vanilla leaf, bunchberry, coolwort, and twinflower. Chanterelle mushrooms push up the duff in fall.

Don't expect to see the river here. The Willamette is on the far side of the valley, meandering through a swampy thicket of vine maple and alder. From 1.7 to 2.4 miles along the trail, however, you can look out across this boggy scrub — a favorite retreat of elk.

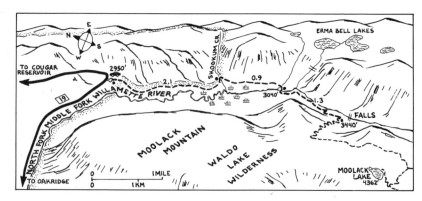

At the 2.1-mile mark cross Skookum Creek on small logs and stepping stones. Then, at the 3-mile mark, cross the outlet creek of the distant Erma Bell Lakes and enter the Willamette's delta at the head of the valley swamp. Looming beside the path are some of the largest red cedar trees in Oregon — many 10 feet in diameter. The river here braids through the woods in channels that change with each flood. Trail maintenance crews do their best to flag a passable route through the confusion, using downed trees as bridges.

Hikers with children should turn back here after investigating the riverside groves. Notice the dainty maidenhair ferns and the numerous water-loving wildflowers: yellow monkeyflower, pink bleeding hearts, and purple larkspur. If you're backpacking, there are plenty of well concealed, flat sites from which to base further explorations.

To continue on to the waterfall, follow gray, diamond-shaped markers across the river. On the far shore, ignore a side trail scrambling up to a disappointing vista. Instead follow the riverside trail — now a narrower and more rugged path, well suited for tracking this raging, frothing, bouldery wilderness river to its lair. After 1.1 miles the trail switchbacks steeply up to a bench. The path then levels for another 0.2 mile before forking. Continue straight 20 yards to a precarious overlook of a churning cascade in the river below — a worthy goal for your hike.

Other Hiking Options

The right-hand fork at the waterfall switchbacks up nearly 1000 feet at a grueling grade. If you keep right at the next 2 trail junctions you'll reach Moolack Lake in 3.6 miles.

Ten-foot-thick red cedar near river crossing.   Opposite: Chanterelle mushrooms.

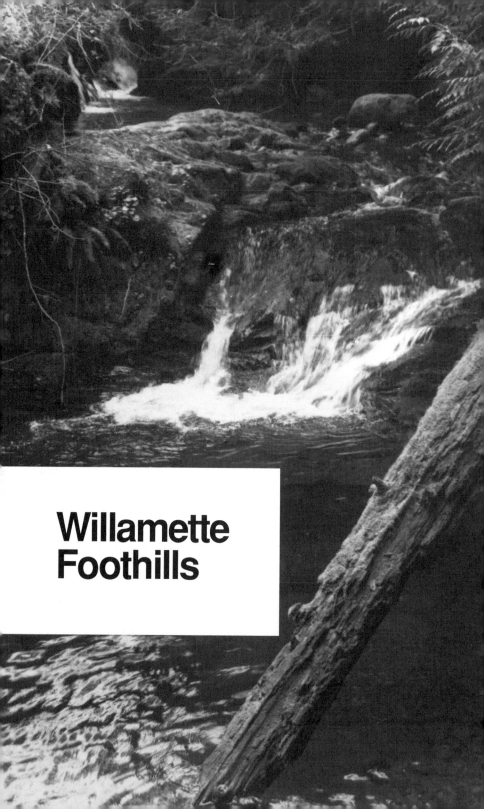

Willamette
Foothills

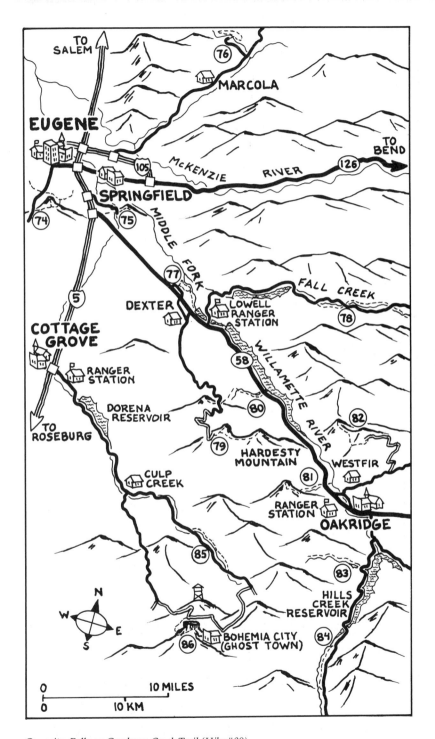

TO
SALEM

76

MARCOLA

EUGENE

TO
BEND

105

McKENZIE RIVER

126

SPRINGFIELD

74

75

MIDDLE FORK

77

FALL CREEK

5

DEXTER

LOWELL
RANGER
STATION

78

COTTAGE
GROVE

RANGER
STATION

58

WILLAMETTE RIVER

TO
ROSEBURG

DORENA
RESERVOIR

80

82

79

HARDESTY
MOUNTAIN

WESTFIR

CULP
CREEK

81

RANGER
STATION

OAKRIDGE

85

83

HILLS
CREEK
RESERVOIR

N
W   E
S

86

BOHEMIA CITY
(GHOST TOWN)

84

0   10 MILES
0   10 KM

Opposite: Falls on Goodman Creek Trail (Hike #80).

74   Spencers Butte

Easy
1.5-mile loop
800 feet elevation gain
Open year-round
Map: Creswell (USGS)

Eugene's skyline is not dominated by buildings, but rather by a long, forested ridge topped with Spencers Butte's haystack-shaped knob. Explore this natural skyline on the South Hills Ridgeline Trail, through forests so thick with Douglas fir and sword fern it's easy to forget city streets lie below.

The Spencers Butte loop is admittedly the steepest and most heavily used part of this trail system, but it's still the best introduction. Children enjoy the challenge of "climbing a mountain" without too much effort, and everyone enjoys the bald summit's 360-degree panorama, extending from Fern Ridge Reservoir to the Three Sisters.

Drive 5 miles south from downtown Eugene on Willamette Street and turn left into the parking lot for Spencers Butte Park. Walk up the broad cement stairs and immediately turn left onto the unmarked summit trail.

After 0.3 miles up through forest, reach a steep grassy slope with views of the Spencer Creek Valley. As in all grassy, open areas on this hike, poison oak abounds along the trail — be careful to avoid these shrubs' shiny, triple leaflets!

In another 0.1 mile the trail disintegrates into a number of steep scramble routes, some with steps. Whichever route you pick, the final pitch to the

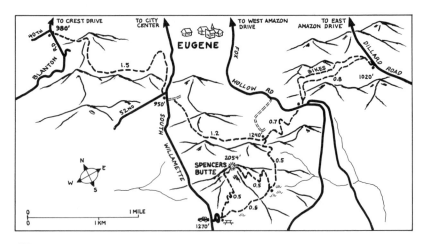

Sighting toward Cottage Grove from Spencers Butte.   Opposite: Summit benchmark.

summit's open, rocky ridge is steep enough to require you to use your hands. A bird's-eye view of the Eugene area waits at the top, with Fern Ridge Reservoir to the west, the Willamette Valley to the north, and the Three Sisters on the eastern horizon. The first white man to scale Spencers Butte was Dr. Elijah White, who came here in 1845 hoping to spy an easy wagon train route through the Cascade Range to the east. He named the peak after the then secretary of war.

To continue the loop hike, descend the far side (the east) of the summit. The trail traverses to the right, splits into several alternate routes, combines, and then switchbacks down through the forest. At a little meadow, an unmarked trail leading to the rest of the Ridgeline Trail takes off to the left; continue straight on the main path to return to the trailhead.

Other Hiking Options

Other portions of the Ridgeline Trail offer fewer views, but the forests are soothingly quiet and the well-constructed paths are nearly level. To hike one or more of these sections one-way, arrange a car shuttle. The trailheads on Blanton Road, South Willamette, Fox Hollow Road, and Dillard Road are clearly marked by hiker-symbol signs.

75   Mount Pisgah

Easy (to summit)
3 miles round-trip
1000 feet elevation gain
Open year-round
Map: Springfield (USGS)

Easy (arboretum tour)
1.6-mile loop
100 feet elevation gain

The first Lane County pioneers climbed this grassy hill between the forks of the Willamette River, viewed the green dales at the end of the Willamette Valley, and named the hill Mount Pisgah, for the Biblical summit from which Moses sighted the Promised Land. The view is still dramatic, and the hike is especially fun when coupled with a stroll through the adjacent arboretum's well-tended trail network.

Just south of Eugene, take the 30th Avenue exit (#189) of Interstate 5 and head for the Texaco gas station on the east side of the freeway. (If you're coming from the north you'll have to drive a mile to 30th Avenue, cross the freeway, and double back.) Just past the station, turn right onto Franklin Boulevard for 0.4 mile, then turn left onto Seavey Loop Road for 1.5 miles, continue straight to cross the Coast Fork Willamette River bridge, and finally turn right for 0.4 mile to the arboretum parking area.

Start hiking uphill on a closed road at a metal gate with the sign, "Mountain Bikes Prohibited." The road/trail climbs through an open oak grassland with bigleaf maples and lots of lush poison oak; stay on the trail to avoid brushing the shiny triple-leaflets of this shrub. Pass under the power lines twice before breaking out into the long summit meadow. Wildflowers here include purple

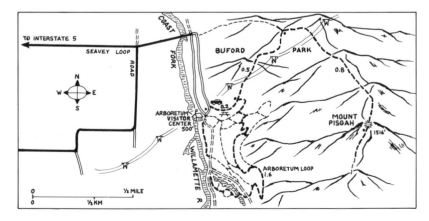

iris, fuzzy cat's ears, and wild strawberries. A bronze sighting pedestal, a memorial to Pleasant Hill author Ken Kesey's son Jed, identifies mountains, rivers, towns, and other landmarks visible from the summit. Bas reliefs on the pedestal's pillars depict more than 300 Oregon fossils.

The adjacent Mt. Pisgah Arboretum offers a variety of easy loop hikes, one of which is suggested on the map. Admission is free; donations are accepted. Children are particularly fond of the bridge over a lilypad slough at the far end of the water garden area, where it's fun to watch for bullfrogs and turtles.

Many of the arboretum's trees and flowers are labeled. Detailed plant lists and trail maps are available in the visitor center beside the parking lot. A hangar-like former barn nearby is used for special events — notably a mushroom show on the last Sunday of October and a wildflower exhibition each May on the Sunday after Mothers' Day. For arboretum information, call 747-3817.

White oak grassland along Mt. Pisgah trail.   *Opposite: Turtle amid water lilies.*

76   Shotgun Creek

Easy
3.4-mile loop
300 feet elevation gain
Open year-round
Map: Marcola (USGS)

In the rustic Mohawk Valley just half an hour from Eugene, this woodsy loop is an ideal first hike for small children. In summer, pack a lunch and end the hike with a picnic beside Shotgun Creek's developed swimming area. In winter, shake off cabin fever by sending the kids around these snowless trails in search of pine cones and orange-bellied newts.

Take the Springfield exit of I-5 and drive east on I-105 to the exit marked "Marcola". Turn left on Marcola Road for 15 miles — continuing 3 miles beyond the town of Marcola — and then turn left at the Shotgun Creek sign. After another 1.6 miles turn right onto the park entrance road, cross a bridge, and park at the picnic area on the left. From November through April, when the Bureau of Land Management closes the park, you'll have to park at a locked gate and walk a few hundred yards to the picnic area.

To begin the suggested loop, hike past the picnic shelters to the Shotgun Creek Trail, following the creek upstream. Mossy bigleaf maple, white-barked alder, and droopy red cedar shade the bank. The path then leaves the creek and climbs gradually through a drier, second-growth forest of Douglas fir and salal. The notches visible in old stumps along the trail were originally fitted with spring-boards to give loggers a place to stand while pulling "misery whips" — two-man crosscut saws.

At the 2.1-mile mark you can turn right at a trail junction for a shortcut to the

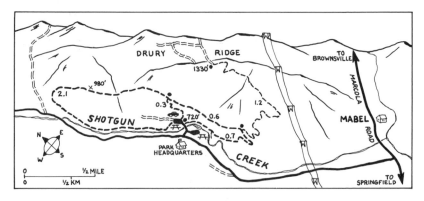

Trail at Shotgun Creek.   Opposite: Rough-skinned newt (salamander).

car. But if you're still going strong, continue straight on the Meadow Loop Trail, which contours through meadowless forest, crossing several rustic footbridges over dry side creeks. After 0.6 mile, ignore the Drury Ridge Trail turnoff to the left (this path climbs to a logging road in a viewless clearcut) and instead continue straight on the Lower Trail. This route switchbacks down to Shotgun Creek and follows the creek to the picnic area.

Middle Fork Willamette River at Elijah Bristow Park.   Opposite: Blackberries.

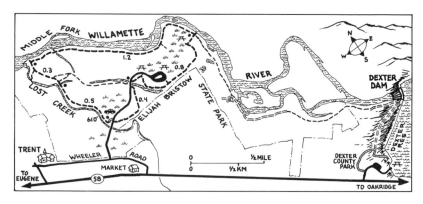

77   Elijah Bristow Park

Easy
3.2-mile loop
Zero elevation gain
Open year-round
Map: Lowell (USGS)

This easy lowland loop along the Middle Fork of the Willamette River near Eugene is pleasant in any season, but it's especially fun in August, when masses of sweet, juicy blackberries ripen along the trail. The state park honors Elijah Bristow, Lane County's first settler. Born in Virginia in 1788, he came to Oregon in 1846 and took up a claim on "a pleasant hill" 5 miles west of here — now the town of Pleasant Hill.

Take the Oakridge exit of Interstate 5 just south of Eugene, drive 7.2 miles east on Highway 58, and turn left at the sign for Bristow Park. After a block turn right on Wheeler Road for 0.7 mile to the park entrance on the left. Don't drive all the way in to the main picnic area. Immediately after crossing the first bridge turn left into a grassy parking area beside Lost Creek. The unmarked trail begins here along the creek. Horses share the path.

The level, well-maintained trail cuts a swath through blackberry patches, at times peeking out across the lazy creek and then dipping into lowland forests of mossy bigleaf maple and occasional red cedars. After crossing a footbridge at the half-mile mark, avoid 2 side trails to the right, continue across a field of Scotch broom, and then avoid a side trail to the left.

Shortly thereafter reach the beachless bank of the swift Willamette River. Alders and tall, honey-scented cottonwood trees line the shore. The trail turns right and winds through these river-edge woods for over a mile.

Finally the path emerges at the main picnic area's lawn. Keep along the riverbank 200 yards to a 4-way trail junction just before a muddy slough. If you turn left 50 feet you'll reach a delightful pebble beach. If you go straight you'll be on the rugged riverside trail to Dexter Dam. Turn right to continue the loop hike.

The loop trail now leaves the river bank and follows an abandoned road through the woods behind the picnic area. Spur trails to the right lead out to picnic lawns. At one point the path briefly joins the paved road in order to cross a slough.

Other Hiking Options

Wear rubber boots if you'd like to continue 2.2 miles along the riverbank from the picnic area to the base of Dexter Dam. Parts of this trail are muddy and may be flooded after heavy rains or when the upstream reservoirs are being drained at the end of summer.

78 Fall Creek

Easy (to Timber Creek)
5.8 miles round-trip
200 feet elevation gain
Open year-round
Map: Saddleblanket Mtn. (USGS)

Moderate (to Rd. 1828, with shuttle)
9 miles one-way
700 feet elevation gain

The trail along this woodsy, low-elevation creek has attractions for each season: fall mushrooms, winter solitude, spring wildflowers, and best of all, summertime swimming holes. For an easy hike, turn back at Timber Creek. Or shuttle a bicycle to the upper trailhead, hike 9 miles of the trail one-way, and shoosh back on 7 miles of pavement to your car.

Start by driving 14 miles east of Interstate 5 on Highway 58. Turn north across Dexter Reservoir at the covered bridge, follow the Jasper-Lowell Road through the town of Lowell (where the road jogs left and then right), continue 1.5 miles to another covered bridge, and turn right on North Shore Road. Follow this paved route 11 miles, around the north side of the reservoir and up Fall Creek. Park at a hiker-symbol sign on the right just before the road crosses the bridge to Dolly Varden Campground.

The trail begins in an old-growth forest greened with a carpet of sword ferns, oxalis, and delicate maidenhair ferns. Fairy bells and bleeding hearts bloom in spring. The trail occasionally dips to creekside gravel beaches, but mostly stays higher on the forested bank, crossing side creeks on log footbridges.

At the 2-mile mark, watch on the left for a large rope in a tree 30 feet above the creek. Swimmers from Big Pool Campground on the opposite shore use this to swing into a deep, blue-green swimming hole. The next mile of trail crosses 3 log footbridges, the last of which spans scenic, 15-foot-wide Timber Creek, a

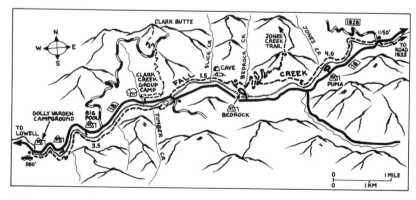

Footbridge beside Fall Creek.   Opposite: Fairy bells.

good place for hikers with children to declare victory and turn back to the car. Hikers who continue — perhaps having arranged a car or bicycle shuttle back from a more distant trailhead — will soon come to an unmarked fork in the trail. Take the right fork, which detours around a dirt road and meets paved Road 18 at its bridge across Fall Creek. Cross the bridge; the trail now continues on the sunnier, drier north side of the valley. Beyond the bridge 0.8 mile the trail passes a grassy knoll with a view of a rocky island and waterfall in the creek below. Shortly thereafter the trail crosses Slick Creek on a high bridge, with a small beach on the right and a nice campsite on the left near Slick Creek Cave.

After another 0.4 mile the trail circumvents Bedrock Campground; avoid side trails to the right. Cross Bedrock Creek and climb 5 long switchbacks to a junction with the Jones Trail, high above Fall Creek. The trail stays high for a mile, then returns to the creek for the final 2.3 miles to the trailhead on gravel Road 1828, a stone's throw from paved Road 18's bridge across Fall Creek.

Other Hiking Options

The Fall Creek Trail continues another 4.7 miles beyond Road 1828. This quiet, scenic upper section starts on the north side of the creek, promptly passes an interesting rock shoreline of water-rounded stone formations, crosses the creek on a long footbridge, and continues on the south bank to trail's end at Road 1833, near that road's junction with paved Road 18.

79

Mount June

Easy (to Mount June)
2.4 miles round-trip
900 feet elevation gain
Open mid-April to mid-December
Map: Mount June (USGS)

Moderate (to Hardesty Mountain)
9.6 miles round-trip
2100 feet elevation gain

An undesignated wilderness in Eugene's backyard, the Hardesty Mountain area is a popular patch of forested ridges and trails. Each year hundreds of hikers march up the 5-mile Hardesty Trail from Highway 58, arduously gaining over 4000 feet in elevation, only to discover that the former lookout site atop Hardesty Mountain is overgrown with young trees, blocking most of the view.

These hikers obviously don't know about Mount June. Not only is it the area's tallest peak, but the panorama from its former lookout site stretches unimpeded from the Willamette Valley to the Three Sisters. What's more, the trail up Mount June is so easy that children can taste the success of "climbing a mountain." And if you continue on the ridgecrest beyond Mount June, you'll reach Hardesty Mountain anyway — by a shorter, easier route.

To find the Mt. June Trailhead, drive 11.4 miles east from Interstate 5 on Highway 58 to Dexter Dam and turn south at a sign for Lost Creek. After 3.7 miles, turn left across a somewhat hidden bridge onto the signed Eagles Rest Road. Follow this paved, one-lane route up 7.8 miles to a fork. Heeding a hiker-symbol pointer here, keep left on Road 20-1-14 for 2.6 miles of pavement and another 3.5 miles of gravel. At the far end of a fenced tree farm, turn left onto Road 1721, and 200 yards later turn left onto steep Road 941 for 0.4 mile to the trailhead sign on the right.

The trail climbs gradually through a Douglas fir forest with a lush understory of sword ferns, shamrock-shaped oxalis, and May-blooming rhododendrons. After 0.7 mile turn right at a trail junction and climb steeply up a ridge toward the summit.

The ridgecrests here are known for their eerie fogs, shafted with rays of sun. But the bare rock of Mt. June's summit usually rises above the fog, providing a view from Mt. Hood to Diamond Peak. The route to Hardesty Mountain is spread before you like a map.

To hike on to Hardesty Mountain, backtrack from the summit to the trail junction and turn right on the Sawtooth Trail. This path goes up and down along the ridgecrest through a dry forest that includes an unusual mixture of chinkapin (with tough leaves and spiny fruits), beargrass (with plumed white blooms), and yew trees (with contorted branches and flat needles). After 0.7 mile, go right at a trail junction. The path now traverses a steep, grassy meadow with a view

Foggy ridge from Mt. June's lookout site.   *Opposite: Enameled pre-1933 trail sign.*

back to Mt. June. The southern horizon is full of Calapooya Mountains, dominated by square-topped Bohemia Mountain (Hike #86).

At the far end of the meadow the trail makes two short switchbacks. From the top of these switchbacks it's easy to scramble up 100 feet to the base of Sawtooth Rock, a 50-foot monolith with a shallow cave in its south base.

Continuing on the main trail, keep left at a marked trail junction, pass a view of Lookout Point Reservoir, and follow the up-and-down ridgecrest another 1.4 miles to a trail junction on the slope of Hardesty Mountain. To make a small loop to the summit, turn left for 0.2 mile to a trail junction on a ridgecrest and follow the right-hand path up to the old lookout site. To return, continue south along the summit ridge and switchback down to the Hardesty Cutoff Trail. Turn right here for 0.2 mile and then turn left on the Sawtooth Trail to return to the car.

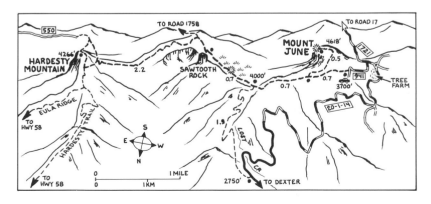

80   Goodman Creek

Easy (to Goodman Creek)
4 miles round-trip
300 feet elevation gain
Open year-round
Map: Mount June (USGS)

Difficult (to Eagles Rest)
13.4 miles round-trip
2100 feet elevation gain
Open mid-March through December

Just half an hour from Eugene, this hike through the forests below Hardesty Mountain can either be an easy walk to a waterfall — popular with kids — or it can be lengthened to a more strenuous trek past Ash Swale Shelter to the viewpoint at Eagles Rest.

Drive Highway 58 to Lookout Point Reservoir. Near milepost 21, park at a pullout marked by a hiker-symbol sign.

The trail starts in an old-growth Douglas fir forest brightened in March and April by the white blooms of trilliums. After 0.2 mile, turn right onto the Goodman Trail, which contours through the woods above an arm of the reservoir. In damp weather watch for rough-skinned newts on the trail — the rugged, orange-bellied "waterdogs" that fascinate children.

The trail crosses a creek, climbs over a small ridge, and descends to a boggy swale. At the 1.9-mile mark, pass a grassy campsite and immediately reach an unmarked trail junction within earshot of falling water. The main path goes right, but take the left fork 50 feet through the vine maple to discover a lovely little waterfall sliding into a swimmable, rock-edged pool overhung with droopy red cedars. Return to the main trail and continue 200 yards to a pebble beach and huge log footbridge across Goodman Creek — a good picnic spot, and the turn-around point for hikers with children. Watch out for the few stinging nettles near the creek.

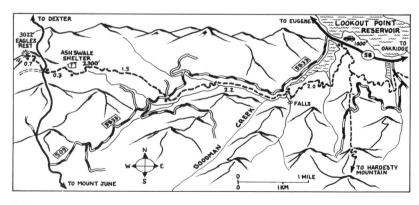

Mossy trail along Goodman Creek.   Opposite: Footbridge near small beach.

If you're continuing, the next 1.2 miles of trail are nearly level, in a delightfully mossy rain forest along the creek. A small gravel road paralleling the trail is mostly out of sight. Next the trail climbs steadily for 1 mile and crosses Road 5833 to a well-marked trailhead for the Eagles Rest Trail. This trail continues to climb through second-growth Douglas fir — at one point crossing a 1989 clearcut — for 1.7 miles to Ash Swale Shelter. The swale beside this solid, 3-sided structure is a skunk cabbage marsh full of frogs.

Beyond the shelter, the trail skirts two large 1989 clearcuts, crosses the paved Eagles Rest Road, and then climbs another 0.7 mile to the dry, rocky summit of Eagles Rest, with its clifftop view across the Lost Creek Valley.

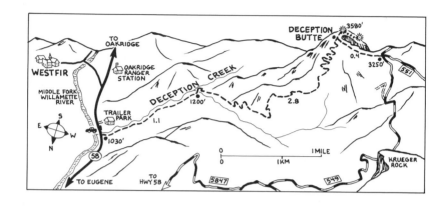

81   Deception Butte

Easy (from Road 549)
1 mile round-trip
300 feet elevation gain
Open April through December
Maps: Holland Pt., Westfir W. (USGS)

Difficult (from Highway 58)
8 miles round-trip
2600 feet elevation gain

For a convenient bit of well-paced exercise, start this quiet forest trail at its lower end on Highway 58. After warming up with a virtually level first mile, the path steepens for 3 miles to a mountaintop meadow overlooking Oakridge and Diamond Peak. On the other hand, if the view interests you more than the exercise, you can start at the upper trailhead on gravel Road 549 and amble up a much easier, half-mile shortcut to the top.

To find the lower trailhead, park on the narrow shoulder of Highway 58 in front of a trailer park at Deception Creek, 0.6 mile west of the Oakridge Ranger Station or 2 miles east of Shady Dell Campground. Walk across the creek on the highway bridge to the trailhead sign on the left.

This lower end of the path sets out through an old-growth hemlock forest carpeted with shamrock-shaped oxalis, but after half a mile you enter a stand of younger Douglas fir. At the 1.1-mile mark, cross a large tributary of Deception Creek on a 50-foot log footbridge.

The trail now climbs in earnest, promptly switchbacking up to an open rock ridge with a view across the valley. Between 1.4 and 1.6 miles switchback through a 1985 clearcut regrown with thimbleberry. From mile 2.7 to 3.0 cross a

Summit of Deception Butte.   Opposite: Thimbleberry.

slightly older clearcut and then climb steeply through woods brightened by pink rhododendrons in early June.

Just 100 feet before the butte's rocky summit, ignore an unmarked trail leading down to the right; this is the path to Road 549. Continue to the summit, a clifftop rock garden of penstemon, paintbrush, and manzanita. However, the only view here is of Krueger Rock across the valley. For a view of Oakridge and Diamond Peak, bushwhack 100 yards past the summit, descending along the ridge to a steep, mossy field of cat's ears.

If you're driving to the upper trailhead, turn off Highway 58 at Shady Dell Campground 6 miles west of Oakridge and take Road 5847 toward Krueger Rock. Follow this one-lane road 4.5 miles to a saddle, and then turn left on Road 549 for 3.2 miles to the intersection of Road 551 in a pass. A sign on the left marks the half-mile trail to Deception Butte.

82   Tire Mountain

Easy
7.6 miles round-trip
800 feet elevation gain
Open May through November
Maps: Westfir E., Westfir W. (USGS)

If you're eager to get a head start on summer, stroll through the wildflower meadows of Tire Mountain, a little-known retreat near Oakridge where the blooms of summer arrive by early June. This hike — easy enough for children — contours 2 miles through sunny meadows with views of Cascade snowpeaks and then climbs through forest to Tire Mountain's former lookout site.

Take the Westfir exit of Highway 58. At the stop sign beside Westfir's covered bridge, continue straight 4.5 miles on paved Road 19. Turn left on gravel Road 1912 for 6.6 steep, winding miles to Windy Pass, go straight onto Road 1910 for 0.4 mile, and then fork right onto Road 1911 for another 0.4 mile to the "Alpine Trail" sign on the left.

After a few hundred yards through a 1975 clearcut, the trail enters a lovely old-growth forest packed with woodland blooms: twin fairy bells, pink bleeding hearts, yellow wood violets, and 5-petaled candyflowers. In another half mile the path traverses the first of a series of steep meadows. Diamond Peak dominates the skyline to the right while Mt. Bachelor and 2 of the Three Sisters cluster to the left. Below are Hills Creek Reservoir and the oak-dotted ridges of Oakridge, surrounded by clearcuts.

At the 1.2-mile mark, turn right at a trail junction in a patch of tall, purple larkspur. The path ducks into the forest for half a mile and crosses 2 small

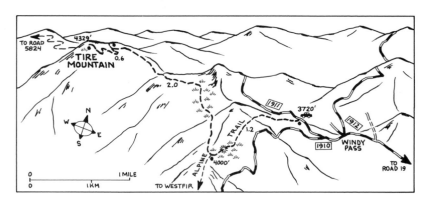

meadows before emerging at the last and largest field, covered each June by a carpet of tiny pink flowers. Also look here for yellow monkeyflower, sunflower-like balsamroot, and blue camas.

If you've brought children you may wish to turn back at this final meadow, trimming the round-trip distance to just 4.2 miles. Otherwise, follow the virtually level path 1.1 miles on through the ridgetop forest to a trail junction on the wooded slope of Tire Mountain. Take the uphill fork, switchbacking to the broad, brushy summit. Trees block much of the view. A few boards remain from the unusual lookout tower that once stood atop the truncated tree in the middle of the summit field.

Tire Mountain is named for Tire Creek, where an early traveler on the old military wagon road to Oakridge left a broken wagon wheel.

Balsamroot blooming in meadow.   Opposite: Junction of Alpine and Tire Mountain trails.

Trail beside Larison Cove.   Opposite: Salal.

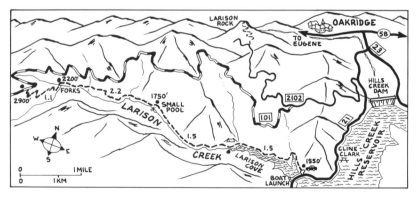

83   Larison Creek

Easy (to small pool)
6 miles round-trip
200 feet elevation gain
Open year-round
Map: Oakridge (USGS)

Moderate (to fork in creek)
10.4 miles round-trip
700 feet elevation gain

This easy trail, hikable even in winter, starts along a sunny shore of Hills Creek Reservoir and then follows a small creek through a deep, forested canyon.

Drive 1.3 miles east of Oakridge on Highway 58 and turn south at the sign for Hills Creek Reservoir. After half a mile, fork right onto paved Road 21 for 3.3 miles. A hiker-symbol sign on the right marks the parking area beside an arm of the reservoir.

The first 1.5 miles of the trail contour around deep, green Larison Cove, cut off from the main reservoir by the road's dike. Only non-motorized boats are allowed on the cove. The rocky hillsides here host sparse Douglas fir and some poison oak; don't let children touch triple-leaved bushes. At the end of the cove the path crosses a side creek and reaches an established picnic/camping area sometimes used by boaters. Cattails fringe the shore.

Beyond the reservoir the trail follows the creek through a cooler, mossier forest of old-growth Douglas fir, red cedar, and twisted yew trees. Lily-white trillium and shamrock-like oxalis bloom here in April, followed by pink rhododendron and yellow Oregon grape in May.

The path climbs very gradually, staying within a stone's throw of the creek. Beyond the reservoir 1.5 miles watch carefully for a small water chute and pool through the trees to your left. Bushwhack 50 feet to this small but pleasant picnic spot, where the creek swirls down a 10-foot-long bedrock slide into a pool so clear you can count the fingerling fish. This makes a good turn-around point for hikers with children.

Beyond the small pool 0.7 mile, the trail climbs away from the creek. Briefly cross a 1976 clearcut at the 4.4-mile mark. Finally return to the creek at another nice picnic site — a pleasant, mossy bower just before the creek forks and the trail begins its switchbacking climb out of the canyon.

Other Hiking Options

With a car shuttle you can hike the entire 6.3-mile trail downhill. To find the upper trailhead, turn off Road 21 onto Larison Rock Road 2102 just below the Hills Creek Dam (1.5 miles from Highway 58). Follow paved Road 2102 for 2 miles, then turn left onto gravel Road 101 for 8.2 winding miles to a hiker-symbol sign on the left. The trail switchbacks steeply down through a raw 1989 clearcut to the creek's fork.

84 Middle Fork Willamette

Easy (with shuttle)
5.1 miles one-way
400 feet elevation gain
Open year-round
Map: Warner Mountain (USGS)

Though deep in the Cascade Range, this stretch of river is still recognizably the grand old Willamette. Tall cottonwoods line the pebbled bank, filling the air with honeyed fragrance. Great blue herons wade the riffles. Mallards start up from oxbow sloughs. Trailside alders show the toothmarks of beaver.

The Forest Service has built more than half of a planned 40-mile Middle Fork Willamette Trail from Hills Creek Reservoir to the river's source at Timpanogas Lake (see Hike #100) — but the completed segments are still separated by gaps. This hike traces the first, lowest section. Because the route parallels paved Road 21, it's easy to shuttle a vehicle to the upper end and hike the trail one way. If you can't bring a second car for the job, bring a bicycle. The 4-mile ride back is all downhill.

Turn off Highway 58 at the sign for Hills Creek Reservoir 1.3 miles east of Oakridge. After half a mile bear right onto Road 21 and follow this route around the reservoir 12 miles. A mile past the Sand Prairie Campground turn right at a hiker-symbol sign and drive 200 yards to the trailhead by the river. The trail is open to motorcycles and horses but they seldom use it, perhaps because of the narrow footbridges over side creeks.

The path starts out between a horse loading area and some gravel piles. After crossing Buck Creek on a 60-foot bridge the trail swings close to the paved road for 0.3 mile — at one point briefly following the shoulder. Then the path strikes

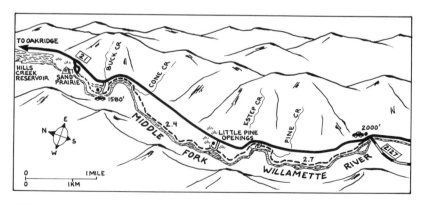

Middle Fork Willamette River.   Opposite: Bigleaf maple.

off through the forest and crosses placid, 8-foot-wide Cone Creek. There's no bridge; hop across on stones as best you can. After spring rains, the river sometimes floods this portion of the path.

By the 1-mile mark you're on the riverbank again in a marvelously diverse forest of cottonwoods and conifers with an understory of horsetail, coltsfoot, and snowberry. Children delight in spotting wildlife here. Kingfishers, mallards, and many other birds frequent the bank. Expect elk in spring and early summer. Beavers are here too, judging from gnawed stumps along the way. The trail even crosses an old gravel bar where lizards scurry.

At Little Pine Openings, 2.4 miles along, the path briefly joins a gravel road, then continues along the riverbank. At the 3-mile mark the river squeezes close to the paved road, wedging the trail in between. The path crosses a dirt road to a campsite here. The final 1.8 miles follow a more isolated stretch of riverbank, passing a nice gravel beach at the foot of an island in the river.

Other Hiking Options

To try a portion of the Middle Fork Willamette Trail that's deeper in the mountains, drive 13 miles on Road 21 past the upper trailhead for this hike. Park at a trailhead opposite the Indigo Spring Campground entrance. A new 7-mile stretch of trail follows the rugged, scenic riverbank up to the Road 2153 bridge at Paddys Valley.

85   Brice Creek

Easy (with shuttle)
5.5 miles one-way
600 feet elevation gain
Open year-round
Map: Rose Hill (USGS)

The newly completed trail along this lovely creek leads past small waterfalls and swimmable pools under the canopy of an old-growth forest. The route is fun for children and open even in winter. A paved road unobtrusively parallels the trail on the creek's opposite shore, making access easy at several points. To hike the entire trail one-way, plan on leaving a shuttle vehicle at the upper trailhead; a bicycle will do fine, since the return ride is all downhill.

Take the Cottage Grove exit of Interstate 5 and follow signs to Dorena Lake. Continue on the main, paved road through Culp Creek and the Disston (bear right at this village) for a total of 21.7 miles from the freeway. A mile past the Umpqua National Forest entrance sign, where the road bridges Brice Creek, look for the trailhead sign on the left. Roadside parking is available 100 feet before the trailhead.

The trail starts on a dry slope but soon plunges into a more typical, mossy old-growth forest of Douglas fir and red cedar. Sword ferns, oxalis, and twinflower thrive here.

At the 1.2-mile mark the trail climbs to a viewpoint on a dramatic cliff above a bend in the creek. Then the path descends to a trail junction. Take a short side trip to the right to inspect the 150-foot-long footbridge to Cedar Creek Campground. Then continue on the main trail.

A quarter mile beyond is a charming, 8-foot waterfall surrounded by smooth rock terraces ideal for sunbathing or picnicking. Children can play on a small beach nearby, while swimmers will find the clear, 15-foot-deep pool beside the terrace tempting. If other picnickers have claimed this spot, however, don't crowd them; the next mile of trail passes half a dozen creekside sites almost as attractive.

The trail climbs to a bluff 300 feet above the creek at the 3.3-mile mark. When the path finally returns to the creek there's a large campsite on the right — a fine spot to take children on a first backpack. Another 200 yards further is the trail junction for Lund Park Campground. A long footbridge crosses the creek to this virtually undeveloped roadside meadow.

Note that Lund Park is not a park. It was once the site of a wayside inn popular with travelers to the Bohemia gold mining district before the turn of the century, and was named for its owners, Alex Lundgren and Tom Parker. With similar

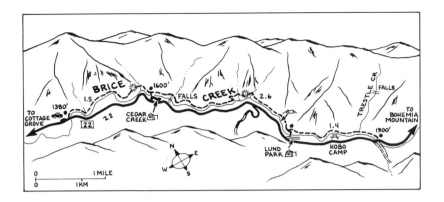

profundity, Brice Creek is a drawling commemoration of Frank Brass, an early prospector who once fell into the stream.

When you continue on the main trail past the Lund Park junction, you'll pass more evidence of the area's mining days. The Vega placer claim is still staked at the mouth of Trestle Creek. Adventurers can bushwhack a mile up this side creek to a hidden waterfall.

The final 0.6 mile of the Brice Creek Trail follows an abandoned, dry flume once used for a power plant at Lund Park. The path ends at the paved road's second bridge across Brice Creek.

Waterfall above Cedar Creek Campground.   Opposite: Footbridge at Lund Park.

86　Bohemia Mountain

Easy
1.6 miles round-trip
700 feet elevation gain
Open mid-June through November
Map: Fairview Pk. (USGS)

Cliff-edged Bohemia Mountain towers above the gold-mining ghost town of Bohemia City. A short steep trail to the top features a view from the Three Sisters to Mt. McLoughlin. Although the hike up usually takes less than an hour — even for hikers with children — you can easily fill a day here by prowling the ghost town, picking huckleberries, or driving up to the 60-foot lookout tower on neighboring Fairview Peak.

Take the Cottage Grove exit of Interstate 5 and follow signs to Dorena Lake. Continue on the main, paved road through the villages of Culp Creek and Disston, and continue straight on the paved road along Brice Creek a total of 30.5 miles from the freeway. Along the way the road number changes from Lane County 2470 to Forest Service 22. Finally, at a pointer for Fairview Peak, turn right onto gravel Road 2212. Follow this route 8.4 miles to Champion Saddle and turn left onto Road 2460, heeding another sign for Fairview Peak. The road now becomes narrow, steep, and rough. Continue carefully 1.1 mile to a 4-way junction at Bohemia Saddle. Park here and walk 100 yards to the left to the signed start of the Bohemia Mountain Trail.

The path climbs a sparsely forested ridge where blue huckleberries ripen in late August. Switchbacks lead to the summit plateau, capped by a layer of tough andesite lava. Thick-leaved stonecrop plants hug the rock. Diamond Peak looms large to the east. The patchwork forests of the Calapooya Mountains stretch in

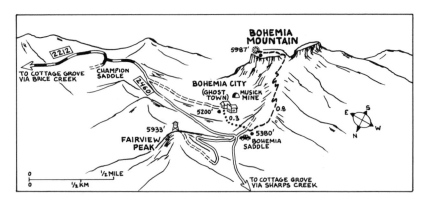

Summit of Bohemia Mountain. Opposite: Building at Bohemia City.

all directions like a rumpled quilt. Far to the northwest are the flats of the Willamette Valley.

The buildings visible at the base of the mountain are the remains of Bohemia City — a boomtown named for James "Bohemia" Johnson, a wandering Czechoslovakian immigrant who discovered gold here in 1863. In the town's heyday from 1880 to 1930, 1750 pounds of gold were mined.

Though the ghost town is on Lane County parkland, the traditional access road from Road 2460 crosses private land and may be gated on a slope where it's difficult for cars to turn around. Mining has not ceased altogether in this area. Hikers need to avoid private land, mining equipment, and dangerous mine shafts.

However, you can still *bushwhack* to the ghost town on public land. Return to the start of the Bohemia Mountain Trail and head east, scrambling 0.3 mile down a steep, brushy hillside to the town's 2 remaining buildings.

For an easier side trip from Bohemia Saddle, drive the steep, 1-mile road to Fairview Peak's climbable fire lookout tower, staffed in summer.

To drive home via a loop, continue west from Bohemia Saddle on Road 2460. This shorter but rougher route to Cottage Grove follows Sharps Creek to the main road at Culp Creek.

Willamette
Pass

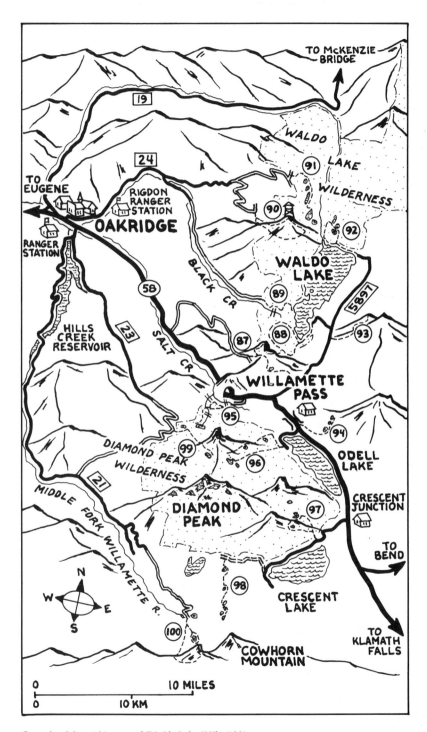

Opposite: Mount Yoran and Divide Lake (Hike #99).

87   Fuji Mountain

Easy (from Road 5833)
3 miles round-trip
950 feet elevation gain
Open mid-July through October
Map: Waldo L. Wilderness (USFS)

Difficult (from Road 5897)
11.2 miles round-trip
2200 feet elevation gain

When a delegation from Eugene's sister city in Japan visited Oregon, officials took them on a hike up Fuji Mountain.

It wasn't a bad choice. The former lookout site atop this cliff-edged peak has a 360-degree view of some of Oregon's greatest treasures: virgin forests, vast Waldo Lake — purest in the world — and pristine snowpeaks from the Three Sisters to Mt. McLoughlin. A popular new shortcut up Fuji Mountain begins on gravel Road 5833. The longer, traditional route from paved Road 5897 provides a more thorough athletic workout.

To take the shorter route, drive 15 miles east of Oakridge on Highway 58. By the railroad trestle between mileposts 50 and 51, turn north onto Eagle Creek Road 5833. After 11.5 miles, park opposite a hiker-symbol sign on the left.

The trail traverses a clearcut for 100 yards, then enters a mountain hemlock forest where blue huckleberries ripen in late August. After 0.3 mile, turn left at a junction. As you climb, the path gradually steepens and the switchbacks shorten. The trees dwindle. Openings of blue lupine permit views of Diamond Peak to the south and Bunchgrass Ridge to the west. Finally follow a ridge to the rocky summit, with its vista of 7-mile-long Waldo Lake.

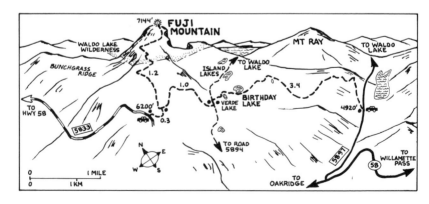

Maiden Peak from Fuji Mountain.   Opposite: Birthday Lake.

To start from the lower trailhead instead, turn off Highway 58 at the sign for Waldo Lake, 3 miles west of Willamette Pass. Follow paved Road 5897 exactly 2 miles to the trailhead sign on the left. Park on the shoulder on the right.

This lower portion of the Fuji Mountain Trail is open to horses and bicycles, though you're unlikely to meet any. The path climbs steeply for 1 mile, then strikes off across a broad, forested benchland. Green, tree-rimmed Birthday Lake, 3 miles from the trailhead, is often warm enough for a dip. Just beyond is a smaller green pool, appropriately named Verde Lake. Continue 0.2 mile to a trail junction and head left for 100 feet to a second junction. This time turn right and climb 1 mile to the summit shortcut trail described above.

88   South Waldo Lake

Easy (to South Waldo Shelter)
3.4 miles round-trip
Zero elevation gain
Open mid-June to early November
Map: Waldo L. Wilderness (USFS)

Moderate (to Black Meadows)
9.8-mile loop
1000 feet elevation gain

Perhaps the prettiest portion of the shoreline trail around mile-high Waldo Lake, this hike starts at a popular sailboat landing and leads past a sandy beach to a shelter in a meadow. More ambitious hikers can add a loop through a remote corner of the Waldo Lake Wilderness, passing Black Meadows and the prodigious huckleberry fields near Bingo Lake. Visit in August for berries; avoid July because of mosquitoes.

Oregon's second largest lake, Waldo covers 10 square miles to a depth of 417 feet. Despite its size the lake has no inlet, leaving its waters so pure and clear they are virtually devoid of plant life. Boaters can watch fish swimming 100 feet deep. The lake is named for Judge John B. Waldo, an early devotee of the Oregon Cascades who trekked from Willamette Pass to Mt. Shasta in 1888.

Turn off Highway 58 at the sign for Waldo Lake, 3 miles west of Willamette Pass. Follow paved Road 5897 for 6.8 miles, turn left at the Shadow Bay Campground sign, and drive 2 miles to the boat ramp parking area.

The trail begins by a water faucet at the north end of the vast parking lot. The path's first half mile is graveled, following the shore of Shadow Bay. Sailboats strike romantic poses in the bay. The growl of powerboats damages the idyll. Despite the ardent pleas of environmentalists, the Forest Service continues to endanger this fragile alpine lake — surrounded on 3 sides by Wilderness — by allowing motors.

At the 1.3-mile mark, reach a sandy beach sheltered by a small wooded island — a nice wading spot on a hot day. After this the trail leaves the lake and skirts a meadow to the shelter, a rustic, 3-sided structure not near the shore.

The loop trail beyond the shelter follows faint paths at times. If you're adventurous, continue on the main trail (following the "High Divide Trail" arrow), cross a large footbridge, and 100 feet later watch for an obscure side trail to the left marked "South Waldo Trail." This path climbs through the woods 1.1 mile to a pass and then descends past a small lake to a 4-way trail junction. Turn right, climb to another wooded pass, dip to a smaller saddle, and then descend steeply for 1 mile to Black Meadows.

The upper end of these meadows is damp, with marsh marigolds and a pond reflecting Fuji Mountain (Hike #87). But as you continue downhill the vale grows drier. Tall grass and the boat-shaped leaves of green hellebore obscure the tread. Continue to a large brown trail junction sign. Turn right, following trail blazes

Waldo Lake's Shadow Bay.   Opposite: South Waldo Shelter.

shaped like exclamation points. Cross a (usually dry) creekbed and look for a cut log, where the tread again becomes clear.

Half a mile beyond Black Meadows the trail crosses a smaller meadow. The tread is faint here, too, but simply follow the meadow to the right to its extreme end.

Next the path enters a first-rate huckleberry patch. Wildfire killed most trees on this hillside; the resulting sunshine makes the berries particularly fat and juicy. Continue purple-fingered past Bingo Lake and over a rise to the Waldo shoreline trail. Turn right and pass a lovely swimming beach en route back to the shelter.

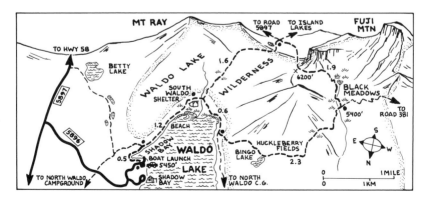

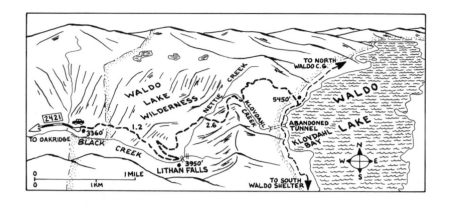

89   Lithan Falls

Easy (to Lithan Falls)
2.4 miles round-trip
600 feet elevation gain
Open mid-April through November
Map: Waldo L. Wilderness (USFS)

Difficult (to Klovdahl Bay)
7.6 miles round-trip
2200 feet elevation gain
Open mid-June through October

A vast glacier capped the Cascade crest during the Ice Age, gouging Waldo Lake's basin and spilling long, snake-like streams of ice down half a dozen valleys to the north and west. When the glacier melted from its mile-high plateau, Waldo Lake was left to choose a single outlet. It opted for a rugged and remote valley to the north. But the huge lake also nearly overflows to the west, into Black Creek's 2000-foot-deep canyon.

In 1912, engineer Simon Klovdahl set out to exploit this coincidence for hydroelectric power and irrigation. He spent 2 years blasting a diversion tunnel from Waldo Lake to the headwaters of Black Creek. When his tunnel didn't work, the project was abandoned to the wilderness.

Today the Black Creek Trail climbs up this dramatic, unspoiled canyon amid old-growth trees 6 feet in diameter. For an easy hike, stop at Lithan Falls' 150-foot series of mossy cascades. For a more challenging trip, continue up from the canyon to Waldo Lake and the headgates of Klovdahl's failed tunnel.

Turn north off Highway 58 at the traffic light in Oakridge. Cross the railroad tracks to a stop sign and turn right on what becomes Salmon Creek Road 24. Follow this paved route for 11 miles to a Y junction. Keep right on Road 24 to the end of pavement in another 3.2 miles, and then continue straight on gravel Road 2421 for 8.2 miles to the trailhead at road's end.

View across Waldo Lake's Klovdahl Bay to Mt. Ray.   *Opposite: Blue huckleberries.*

The trail begins in a 1970 clearcut, but soon passes the Waldo Lake Wilderness sign and enters a magnificent old-growth forest of mountain hemlock and red cedar. Look for white woodland blooms: trilliums in May, tiny twinflower in June, and star-flowered smilacina in July.

After 1.2 miles the path switchbacks at the base of Lithan Falls, a nice picnic spot and the turning-back point for hikers with children. This turbulent cascade is also known as Lillian Falls.

After the falls the trail climbs steeply 0.7 mile before leveling off in a densely forested upper valley. Rhododendrons bloom here in June. Then the path climbs again, traversing a sunny rockslide with views across the canyon. Duck into the scenic, hidden glen of Klovdahl Creek, switchback up through a forest full of huckleberry bushes, and finally descend to the shore of Klovdahl Bay.

Waldo Lake is so large and wild it feels like a fjord in Alaska's Inside Passage. Waves crash on boulders. Gray lichen beards the snow-bent trees. The far shore, miles away, is a silhouette of forest-furred ridges.

Follow the shoreline trail half a mile to the right to view the rotting headgates of Klovdahl's tunnel, which nearly succeeded in reducing this mighty lake to a reservoir.

90 Waldo Mountain Lookout

Difficult
8.5-mile loop
2000 feet elevation gain
Open July through October
Map: Waldo L. Wilderness (USFS)

Waldo Mountain's staffed lookout building features a view from Mt. Hood to Diamond Peak, with Waldo Lake a pool of melted silver at your feet. Visit the lookout on a loop hike that returns through Waldo Meadows, hip-deep in wildflowers. A short, optional side trip leads to Upper Salmon Lake and a small waterfall.

To find the trailhead, turn north off Highway 58 at the traffic light in Oakridge. Cross the railroad tracks to a stop sign and turn right on what becomes Salmon Creek Road 24. Follow this paved route for 11 miles to a Y, and veer left onto Road 2417 for 6 miles. Half a mile after Road 2417 turns to gravel, fork to the right onto Road 2424 and drive 3.7 miles to a hiker-symbol sign on the right marking the trailhead.

After 200 yards the trail forks; this is the start of the loop. Turn left and climb through a mixed forest of mountain hemlock and true firs. As you ascend, the slope grows drier. The lush understory of vanilla leaf and coolwort yields to rhododendron, which in turn gives way to drought-resistant beargrass. Turn right at a junction 1.9 miles along the trail and continue steeply uphill another mile to the towerless lookout building.

The Three Sisters line up to the south. Directly across Waldo Lake are The Twins (Hike #93) and Maiden Peak. To the right, Diamond Peak rises above Fuji Mountain (Hike #87). If you set down your backpack while enjoying the view,

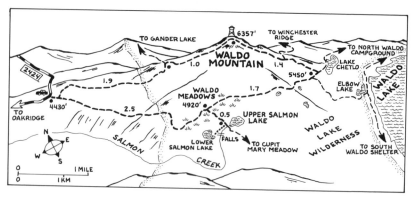

Waldo Mountain Lookout.   Opposite: Falls near Upper Salmon Lake.

be forewarned that the lookout's half-tame ground squirrels probably will ransack its pockets for goodies.

To continue, head toward Waldo Lake down an open, rocky ridge. Ignore a faint side trail to the left halfway down. At the base of the mountain turn right at a simple T junction marked with no fewer than 8 signs. After another 300 yards ignore a left fork for Elbow Lake. Go straight for 1.4 miles and enter Waldo Meadows. The tread can be obscure here amidst the profusion of false hellebore, brown coneflower, red paintbrush, and purple aster. Simply continue through the middle of this long, narrow meadow for 0.3 mile to a campsite (roped off for restoration) and a trail junction at the edge of meadow.

If you'd like to take a short side trip to shallow Upper Salmon Lake, turn left here, cross the meadow, and hike half a mile through the woods. To find Salmon Creek's 20-foot waterfall, follow the lake's outlet 150 yards downstream.

Back at the Waldo Meadows junction, follow the "Salmon Lake Road" pointer 2.5 miles, gradually descending along a hillside to your car.

Other Hiking Options

Backpackers in particular will be tempted to extend this loop down to Waldo Lake. From the trail junction at the eastern base of Waldo Mountain, it's only 0.8 mile to Elbow Lake, near Waldo Lake's shore. To return on a loop, follow the shoreline trail 2.4 miles north to Waldo Lake's outlet and turn left on a 1.2-mile trail back to the base of Waldo Mountain via Chetlo Lake.

North end of Long Lake.   *Opposite: Pinesap, a leafless saprophyte of forest duff.*

91   Eddeeleo Lakes

Moderate
9.2 miles round-trip
700 feet elevation gain
Open mid-June through October
Map: Waldo L. Wilderness (USFS)

Ed, Dee, and Leo were 3 early Forest Service employees who hiked into this string of lakes to plant fish. Hikers have been carrying fish the other way ever since. Note that the path leads *downhill* to the lakes, leaving the elevation gain for the return trip. Along the way, the route emerges once from the mountain hemlock forests for a view of the Three Sisters. Expect rhododendron blooms in June, buzzing mosquitoes in July, and delicious blue huckleberries in August.

Drive Highway 58 to Oakridge and turn north at the town's traffic light. Cross the railroad tracks to a stop sign and turn right on what becomes Salmon Creek

Road 24. Follow this paved route for 11 miles to a Y, veer left onto Road 2417 for 10.9 miles, and then turn left onto Road 254 at a "Winchester Trail" arrow. After just 0.3 mile on this spur, park at a wide spot on the right. If the trailhead sign is missing, watch for the sign's *post*.

Huckleberry bushes line the first, level portion of the trail. Turn left after 0.8 mile, and then, at a junction 0.3 mile beyond, follow the sign for Taylor Burn to the right. After following this trail downhill half a mile, watch for a short side trail to the left. This leads 30 feet to a clifftop viewpoint overlooking Fisher Creek's forested canyon. On the horizon are Irish Mountain and the tops of the Three Sisters.

The trail continues downhill, crosses Lower Quinn Lake's outlet creek (the lake itself is visible through the trees to the right) and then climbs to a trail junction. Take the right-hand fork, even though it may have no sign. In half a mile this path forks again; the right fork loops past the shore of Upper Quinn Lake, while the left fork is a slightly shorter bypass. The routes soon rejoin and continue together to a meadow at the start of Long Lake.

Although the trail parallels Long Lake and then Lower Eddeeleo Lake for most of the next 2.5 miles, it stays in dense woods away from the shoreline. To get views of the lakes you have to watch for short side trails leading through the rhododendrons to the brushy shore. The 2 most scenic accesses are at the end of Long Lake, where a campsite looks across the lake to a tall cliff, and at the start of Lower Eddeeleo Lake, where a faint side trail on the left descends to the outlet creek and continues 200 yards to a lovely lakeshore picnic site with a view of Waldo Mountain (Hike #90).

Other Hiking Options

For a 16-mile backpacking loop, continue 2.4 miles to the outlet of Waldo Lake, follow the Waldo Shore Trail 2.4 miles south to Elbow Lake, turn right for 0.8 mile, turn right for 300 yards, head left toward Waldo Mountain for half a mile, and then turn right on the Winchester Ridge Trail for 5.7 miles to the car.

Backpackers should plan on only using camp stoves; campfires are banned within 100 feet of water, yet rhododendron thickets make tenting difficult outside the few established sites near lakes. Use low-impact camping techniques and dispose of waste water well away from lakes.

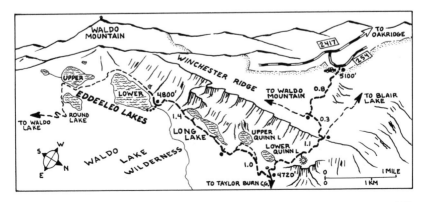

92

Rigdon Lakes

Moderate
8-mile loop
200 feet elevation gain
Open mid-June through October
Map: Waldo L. Wilderness (USFS)

Just 2.4 miles from the North Waldo Campground, the Rigdon Lakes are a popular, easy destination — just right for hikers with children. But before you join the crowds turning back at Upper Rigdon Lake, consider continuing on this remarkably level 8-mile loop. Not only is the longer route still manageable for older children, but it also adds a number of worthwhile attractions: a secluded bathing beach, Waldo Lake's outlet river, and an optional bushwhack up to Rigdon Butte's panoramic view.

Turn off Highway 58 at the "Waldo Lake" sign 3 miles west of Willamette Pass. Drive 13 miles on paved Road 5897, following signs to the Boat and Swim Area parking lot at North Waldo Campground. Park on the right-hand side of the lot near the sign for the Waldo Lake Trail.

Near the start of the main trail a horse path joins from the right, and then a shoreline trail joins from the left. Avoid the temptation to take the shoreline path. Although it offers better views of Waldo Lake, it deadends in less than a mile.

Continue straight on the Waldo Lake Trail through a classic High Cascades forest of lichen-draped mountain hemlock. The greenish-gray lichen is *Usnea,* or old man's beard. Lichens consist of fungi that capture and parasitize green algae. The algae gets its nutrients solely from the air and the rain — and only survives where these are pure. Lichen cannot survive under snow, either; note how the first 6 feet of the tree trunks are bare, indicating the winter snow depth.

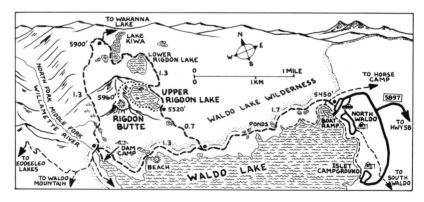

Upper Rigdon Lake and Maiden Peak from Rigdon Butte.   Opposite: Waldo Lake Trail.

The Waldo Lake Trail has disappointingly few views of its 10-square-mile namesake. Instead the trail passes half a dozen lilypad ponds in the woods. After 1.7 miles, turn right at an obvious (but possibly unmarked) trail junction and hike 0.7 mile to Upper Rigdon Lake. The main trail skirts the lake on the right, but a fisherman's trail also follows the shoreline to the left, passing the lake's 2 islands. Due to heavy use, parts of the bank have been roped off for restoration.

The rocky summit of Rigdon Butte is a worthwhile 0.6-mile detour if you're up to the steep, cross-country scramble, because it offers a panoramic view above this area's dense forests. Start from the north shore of Upper Rigdon Lake (near the larger island), scramble up a bluff, and then head left to a cliff-edged promontory overlooking the Rigdon Lakes and the whole of Waldo Lake. To the north are the Three Sisters and — on a clear day — the tip of Mt. Hood. The rumbling railroad sound you hear is the North Fork Middle Fork Willamette River, deep in the canyon to the west.

Back on the loop trail, continue past Lower Rigdon Lake and long, narrow Lake Kiwa to a trail junction. Turn left and hike 1.3 miles through patches of rhododendrons (blooming in June) and huckleberries (ripe in August). Then reach a trail junction at the rushing, 10-foot-wide outlet of Waldo Lake — the North Fork Middle Fork Willamette. The loop continues to the left, but first take a 0.2-mile detour, following the river up to primitive Dam Camp on Waldo Lake.

When you continue on the loop, you'll pass a lovely lakeshore beach after 0.7 mile. This secluded stretch of sand is just the place to wash off the trail's dust with a swim. A rocky peninsula nearby serves for sunbathing. Then it's back to the loop and 2.3 miles to the car.

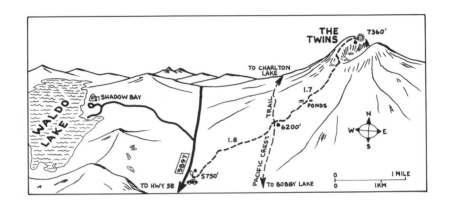

THE
TWINS   7360'

TO CHARLTON
LAKE

SHADOW BAY

WALDO
LAKE

1.7
PONDS

6200'

PACIFIC CREST TRAIL

1.6

5897

5750'

TO HWY 58

TO BOBBY LAKE

N
W   E
S

0   1 MILE
0   1KM

View of South Twin fron North Twin.   Opposite: Mountain hemlock burl.

93   The Twins

Moderate
6.6 miles round-trip
1600 feet elevation gain
Open mid-July through October
Map: Waldo L. Wilderness (USFS)

Admittedly, Maiden Peak is the most popular viewpoint hike east of Waldo Lake. But why join the crowds trudging up 2900 feet in 11.6 miles when you can gain a similar view for about half the effort on the less well-known trail to The Twins? From the airy top of this volcano, vast Waldo Lake sprawls through the forests at your feet while the peaks of the Central Oregon Cascades march along the horizon. Like its bigger sister, Maiden Peak, The Twins is a geologically recent cinder cone with broad, forested flanks and a cute summit crater. The Twins earns its name because its crater rim is cleft, producing a distinctive silhouette.

Drive Highway 58 to the Waldo Lake turnoff 3 miles west of Willamette Pass, head north on paved Road 5897 for 6.2 miles, and park at the "Twin Peaks Trail" sign on the right.

At first the trail climbs very gradually through a dry forest of lodgepole pine, mountain hemlock, and red huckleberry bushes. Cinders and volcanic ash from the volcano's eruptions leave the soil porous.

After 1.6 miles cross the Pacific Crest Trail and begin climbing more steeply. Pass a 100-foot snowmelt pond and then a number of smaller tarns — many dried to mere grassy basins. At this elevation the forest changes to mountain hemlock. Watch for trunks that zigzag, forever locked in deep knee-bends from the snow burdens of winters past. Snow reaches 12 feet deep here, judging from the gray-green *Usnea* lichen that beards trees only above that height.

At the 2.9-mile mark, climb onto red cinder sand of the crater rim, where views south to Diamond Peak commence. Follow the rim clockwise amid wind-gnarled whitebark pines to the highest point of the north Twin. This is one of the Cascades' few viewpoints with a full-length vista of 7-mile-long Waldo Lake. To the north are Charlton Lake and the peaks of the Three Sisters Wilderness.

For a look east, bushwhack 100 feet further along the crater rim to red lava cliffs marking the headwall of a vanished Ice Age glacier. Below are the vast, often partly dry, lakes and reservoirs of Central Oregon.

If you're up to a short cross-country jaunt, cross an open saddle and climb The Twins' north summit. From here you can sight across Bobby Lake to Maiden Peak, and across Gold Lake to Diamond Peak. On the way down, stop in the crater basin's peaceful meadow. Tiny white partridgefoot and pink elephant's head bloom here in late July.

94   Rosary Lakes

Easy
7 miles round-trip
800 feet elevation gain
Open late June to early November
Map: Waldo L. Wilderness (USFS)

Blue beads on a mountain's necklace, the Rosary Lakes sparkle along this popular portion of the Pacific Crest Trail beside Maiden Peak. If you're hiking with children, you can shorten the trip to 5.4 miles by stopping at the first, largest lake. Just don't expect solitude, especially on crowded summer weekends. Nor is this a lonely place to backpack. Since it's the only campable area for miles along the PCT, tents have worn the lakeshores brown.

Turn off Highway 58 at a hiker-symbol sign 0.3 mile east of the Willamette Pass Ski Area, immediately turn right at a highway maintenance gravel shed, and pull into the Pacific Crest Trail parking area.

Climb the stairs and, after a few yards, turn right on the PCT. The first 2 miles of the trail climb very gradually along a forested slope without a single switchback or satisfactory viewpoint. Squint through the forest to glimpse snowy Diamond Peak and huge Odell Lake. At times Southern Pacific trains can be heard across the lake. It's hard to imagine the 1000-foot-thick Ice Age glacier that gouged Odell Lake's basin. The ice would have buried the PCT and connected with a smaller side glacier from the Rosary Lakes' basin. With the ice gone, that side valley has been left hanging 700 feet above Odell Lake.

This part of the trail is a good place to watch for prince's pine, a small pinkish wildflower that blooms in July. Its dark green leaf-whorls are the dominant ground cover here. Also notice the subalpine firs. Usually spire-shaped to shed

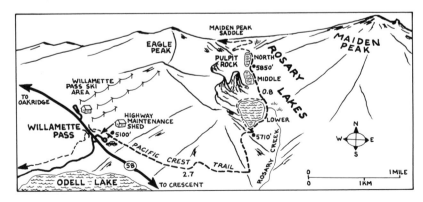

Pulpit Rock from North Rosary Lake.   *Opposite: Subalpine fir branches.*

snow, they have grown huge on this protected slope. Recognize them by their tidy, bluish branches, arranged with a geometric precision that makes neighboring Douglas fir branches look sloppy.

After 2 miles, switchback left into the Rosary Lakes' valley. The trail levels through mountain hemlock woods, skirts a rockslide inhabited by peeping pikas ("rock rabbits"), and switchbacks up to Lower Rosary Lake. The crag beyond the lake is Pulpit Rock, while the low mountain to the right is Maiden Peak. This is the only lake of the cluster ringed by an established fisherman's trail.

Follow the PCT around the lake to the right, cross the outlet creek, and climb through the woods to Middle Rosary Lake. North Rosary Lake is just beyond, separated from the middle lake only by a severely overused campsite with a picnic table.

If you need more exercise, continue 1.1 mile up the PCT to Maiden Peak Saddle. Though the pass is wooded, there are views south to Odell and Crescent Lakes along the way.

95 Diamond Creek Falls

Easy (to Diamond Creek Falls)
3.4-mile loop
400 feet elevation gain
Open May through November
Map: Diamond Pk. Wilderness (USFS)

Moderate (to Vivian Lake)
8 miles round-trip
1600 feet elevation gain
Open mid-June through October

Waterfalls! This stroll starts at magnificent Salt Creek Falls, the state's second tallest, and loops along a canyon rim to lacy Diamond Creek Falls, hidden in a mossy grotto. For a longer hike, continue up a steep trail past churning Fall Creek Falls to Vivian Lake and its tranquil reflection of Mt. Yoran.

Turn off Highway 58 at the sign for Salt Creek Falls (5 miles west of Willamette Pass or 1 mile east of the highway tunnel), and follow the paved entrance road to a turnaround with an information kiosk, restrooms, and picnic tables. Park here and walk 100 feet past the kiosk to an overlook of 286-foot Salt Creek Falls. The falls have cut a dramatic canyon in the edge of a High Cascades basalt flow.

To start the loop hike, follow a concrete pathway upstream, cross Salt Creek on a footbridge, and look for a small sign directing hikers 200 feet through the woods to a well-marked trail junction. Turn right and climb 0.2 mile to a viewpoint of Salt Creek's canyon. Here the trail crosses rock worn smooth by Ice Age glaciers. Notice the honeycomb-shaped fracture pattern characteristic of basalt.

In another 200 yards a short side trail to the left leads to Too Much Bear Lake, a brushy-shored pond. Continue on the main trail 1.2 miles, passing numerous viewpoints, profuse rhododendrons (blooming in June), and 2 small clearcuts before reaching the signed turnoff for Diamond Creek Falls on the right. Take this steep, 0.2-mile side trail down to a footbridge and through a narrow canyon

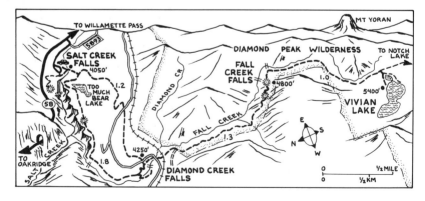

to a misty grotto below the fan-shaped, 100-foot cascade. A surprising mix of lowland wildflowers, watered and cooled by the falls, bloom throughout summer in this hidden glen. Look for scarlet salmonberry blossoms, yellow monkeyflowers, and pink bleeding hearts among the ferns.

Then return to the main trail and switchback up past another viewpoint to a trail junction. If you're hiking with children, turn left here to complete the loop to the car. The 1.2-mile return route crosses a gravel road twice. If you're headed on to Vivian Lake, however, turn right. This path crosses Diamond Creek on a road's cement bridge, ducks through the woods for 300 yards, crosses the Southern Pacific tracks, and climbs into the Diamond Peak Wilderness.

The trail steepens as it climbs, always within earshot of Fall Creek. Beyond the railroad tracks 1.1 mile, reach the first viewpoint of Fall Creek Falls. Continue 0.2 mile to the second, superior overlook of this churning, twisting, 40-foot cascade.

The path stays close to the scenic mossy, tumbling creek for most of the next mile up to the Vivian Lake turnoff. Turn right, cross a meadow, and keep to the right-hand shore of this shallow lake for the view of Mt. Yoran's chunky monolith. In August, fields of ripe blue huckleberries surround the lake.

Salt Creek Falls. Opposite: Reflection of Mt. Yoran in Vivian Lake.

96   Yoran Lake

Moderate
10.8-mile loop
1300 feet elevation gain
Open late June through October
Map: Diamond Pk. Wilderness (USFS)

This woodsy lake, with 2 small islands and a view of Diamond Peak, is a worthy destination even if you merely hike up the 4.3-mile Yoran Lake Trail and return the same way. But if you have some pathfinding skills you can bushwhack 800 yards beyond Yoran Lake through open, level country to the Pacific Crest Trail. And from the PCT you can return on a loop past half a dozen wilderness lakes and ponds.

Just east of the Willamette Pass summit, turn off Highway 58 at the "West Odell Lake Campgrounds" sign. Follow paved Road 5810 for 1.8 miles to a Yoran Lake Trail sign and pull into the parking area on the right.

The trail immediately crosses the Southern Pacific tracks and climbs into a dense forest of mountain hemlock and true fir. Go straight at a 4-way trail junction and climb steadily for 3 miles to a nameless but pleasant green lake on the left. After another half mile, cross Yoran Lake's outlet creek. This rocky torrent dries up by July, when blue lupine and wild strawberry bloom along its meadowed banks.

A half mile beyond, reach an obscure trail junction at the edge of another (dry) creek. The Yoran Lake Trail ducks across the creek on a log and then bypasses Karen Lake. For a better look at Karen Lake, take the more obvious left-hand path, following the (dry) creek up to the lakeshore. Then take a rough fisherman's trail 100 yards around to the right to return to the main path.

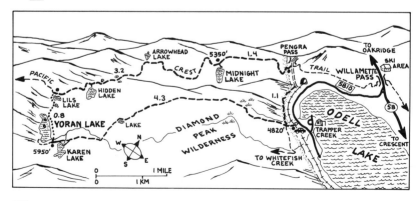

Diamond Peak from Yoran Lake.   Opposite: Pond reflection along trail.

Just beyond Karen Lake, when Yoran Lake peeks through the trees to the right, the trail forks. The left branch leads to a small beach and an overused campsite. The smaller, right-hand fork ends at the lake's outlet, with a view across the lake to Diamond Peak's red-and-black-banded crags.

If you're heading for the PCT, take this right-hand fork, cross the outlet, and bushwhack along the shore almost to the far end of Yoran Lake. Opposite the second small island cross a small inlet creek and come to a campsite on a low bench.

Leave the lakeshore here, following your compass true north (20 degrees *left* of magnetic north). In the first 300 steps you'll cross a meadow, crest a small rise, and reach a pond. In another 150 steps you'll reach Lils Lake. The PCT is in the woods on the far shore. Bushwhack left around the lake to a low cliff on the far side. Then walk north away from the lake 100 steps to the PCT's obvious, 3-foot-wide tread.

Once on the PCT, it's an easy, 4.6-mile downhill roll to Pengra Pass, where the trail meets a dirt road. Follow the road 0.4 mile to the right, and then fork to the right on a trail marked by blue diamonds (for skiers). In 0.6 mile this path intersects the Yoran Lake Trail; turn left to your car.

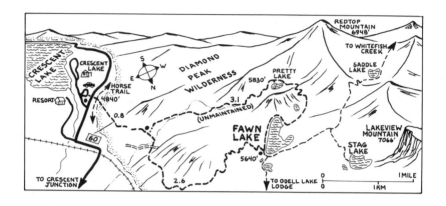

97   Fawn Lake

Moderate
7.3-mile loop
1000 feet elevation gain
Open late June through October
Map: Diamond Pk. Wilderness (USFS)

An oasis in the dry lodgepole pine forests blanketing the High Cascades' eastern slope, Fawn Lake is one of the most popular destinations in the Diamond Peak Wilderness. Alas, popularity has left many of the trails here trammeled to dust. There is one exception: an unmaintained path via Pretty Lake. To make a loop, the suggested route climbs to Fawn Lake on the easy, well-graded trail from Crescent Lake and then returns on this quieter, more difficult path.

Turn off Highway 58 at the "Crescent Lake Campgrounds" sign in Crescent Junction (7.3 miles east of Willamette Pass). Follow paved Road 60 for 2.2 miles, turn right at a pointer labeled "Camping," and in another half mile turn left onto the Crescent Lake Campground entrance road. At the first exit to the right, drive to the far end of a huge parking lot (built for boat trailers) and park by the Fawn Lake Trail sign.

The trail crosses the paved road and a horse trail before heading up past lodgepole pines and aromatic manzanita bushes into the Wilderness. The trail traverses without a single switchback, gaining elevation at a gradual, steady grade. After a mile, cross an abandoned road and enter cooler woods with Douglas fir and the small pinkish blooms of prince's pine. Eventually the hot pine woods return, making it all the more pleasant to reach Fawn Lake's

Pretty Lake.   Opposite: Driftwood at Fawn Lake.

shimmering waters. The craggy peak across the lake is Lakeview Mountain, while the rounded summit to the left is Redtop Mountain.

At the lakeshore the main trail turns right toward a severely overused campsite with a picnic table. But if you turn *left* you'll find yourself on a much quieter, fainter shoreline path. This is the unmaintained route to Pretty Lake. Return via this loop only if you have some skill at pathfinding — and if you don't mind stepping over a few small logs.

The path circles halfway around Fawn Lake and then curves away from the shore through a sparse stand of lodgepole pine; watch for i-shaped blazes on the trunks. Beyond the lake 0.3 mile the trail climbs a more densely forested ridge, faintly switchbacking 3 times to a low pass. Here the path veers left and descends 0.3 mile to an old-fashioned enamel sign announcing Pretty Lake. The shallow, moss-banked pool, 100 feet to the left of the trail, offers a distant reflection of Lakeview Mountain.

Beyond Pretty Lake the path descends a manzanita-covered slope with a view of cone-shaped Odell Butte. After a steady, 2.3-mile downhill grade, rejoin the main trail to Crescent Lake and turn right. Notice that this unmarked junction is only clear when hiking in this direction. Do not try to hike this loop in reverse, as fallen trees make this end of the Pretty Lake Trail virtually invisible from below.

Other Hiking Options

Stag Lake, overtowered by Lakeview Mountain's cliffy face, is an excellent side trip. Turn right at the shore of Fawn Lake and in 0.2 mile keep left at the Odell Lake turnoff. After another mile of gradual climbing, turn right on the 0.4-mile side trail to Stag Lake.

Windy Lakes

Moderate
11.2 miles round-trip
900 feet elevation gain
Open mid-July to mid-October
Map: Diamond Pk. Wilderness (USFS)

If you love mountain lakes, try this walk through the High Cascade forests south of Diamond Peak. The path passes 6 major lakes and 22 ponds. Some have lilypads or meadowed banks; others feature rock outcroppings or forested peninsulas. The Third Windy Lake even has a long sandy beach suitable for swimming.

The suggested route begins at the primitive dirt road to Summit Lake. This is not the most heavily used route to the Windy Lakes. Most hikers innocently start at the large developed trailhead beside Crescent Lake. To be sure, that steep, dusty alternative is half a mile shorter, but it's crowded with horses and it passes no ponds at all.

Turn off Highway 58 at the "Crescent Lake Campgrounds" sign in Crescent Junction and follow paved Road 60. After 2.2 miles, the road turns right at an intersection; follow the pointer labeled "Camping." Exactly 5 miles beyond this intersection, turn right onto an *easily overlooked dirt road* marked "6010 Summit Lake." (If you pass a large sign for the Windy/Oldenburg Trail, you've missed the dirt road by half a mile.) Road 6010 is steep and rutted, but passable for passenger cars except in very wet weather. Follow this road 3.9 miles to a sign for the Meek Lake Trail on the left. Mountain bikes are allowed on the path, but are uncommon.

The trail descends 0.2 mile to a footbridge over Summit Creek and then begins a long, very gradual ascent through lichen-draped mountain hemlock forests. After 0.5 mile a large fork to the right leads to a campsite on a peninsula of deep Meek Lake. Continue on the fainter left fork. The ponds commence at the 1.2-mile mark and pop up along the trail every few hundred yards from then on.

After 2.9 miles turn left at a trail junction at the head of a long, green lake. Continue 1.6 miles, passing North Windy Lake, to an unmarked trail junction beside East Windy Lake. The right-hand fork deadends at a peninsula campsite, so turn left. In 300 yards you'll reach a marked junction with the heavily used trail from Crescent Lake; turn right, following the "S. Windy Lake" pointer.

This route leads around the end of East Windy Lake (with the barest glimpse of Diamond Peak, the hike's only mountain view) and heads through the woods to the Third Lake's delightful, heather-banked beach. The water is usually warm

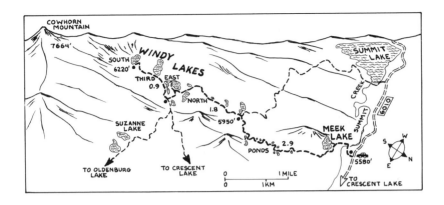

enough for bathing, but the beach really is windy much of the time because the lake is set right at the Cascade crest.

The trail deadends in another half mile at South Windy Lake, the greenest of all, in a deep, forested basin. Return by the same trail.

Third Windy Lake.   Opposite: Deer tracks on lake beach.

99   Divide Lake

Moderate
8 miles round-trip
1200 feet elevation gain
Open July through October
Map: Diamond Pk. Wilderness (USFS)

Diamond Peak does indeed have the kind of idyllic alpine scenery that draws crowds to more famous Oregon peaks. But here most of the alpine idylls are packed into one miniature cove: the little-known Divide Lake basin between Diamond Peak and Mt. Yoran. If you have extra energy after hiking up to Divide Lake, an 0.8-mile climb leads to a pass with a view across Central Oregon.

Turn off Highway 58 at the sign for Hills Creek Reservoir (1.3 miles east of Oakridge). After half a mile on Road 21, continue straight at an intersection onto Road 23. Follow this route for 15.6 miles of pavement and another 3.9 miles of gravel to a pass beside Hemlock Butte. Turn left at a hiker-symbol sign immediately beyond the pass, drive 200 yards on a spur road, and park at the Vivian Lake Trailhead.

The trail starts in a clearcut with a view ahead to Diamond Peak's snowy ridges and Mt. Yoran's massive plug. Then enter uncut mountain hemlock woods with loads of blue huckleberries in August. After 0.6 mile ignore the Diamond Peak Tie Trail branching off to the right; this connector was recently completed to allow backpackers to circumnavigate Diamond Peak entirely on trail. A few hundred yards beyond, reach the start of Notch Lake. Continue to the lake's far end for the best overview of this scenic, rock-rimmed pool.

At a trail junction 0.2 mile beyond the lake, turn right onto the Mt. Yoran Trail. This path climbs in earnest for 1.6 miles before leveling off along a ridgecrest.

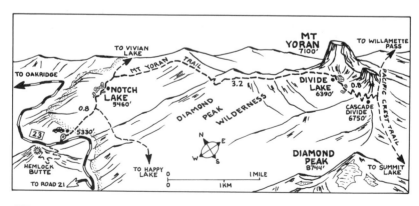

Mt. Yoran from Divide Lake.   *Opposite: Boletus mushroom.*

The ridge has occasional views both south to Diamond Peak and north across Salt Creek's forested valley. After a mile along the ridge, Mt. Yoran's massive monolith suddenly appears above the woods ahead. Then the trail contours to the right across a rockslide to Divide Lake.

Though very small, this blue-green lake is fortuitously situated to reflect 3 different peaks from different shores. Walk around the shore to the right, following a pointer labeled "Pacific Crest Trail." Notice how the rock at the far end of the lake has been rounded and polished by the Ice Age glacier that carved this scenic basin. A bit further along the trail, find a second heather-rimmed lake.

If you're backpacking, be a sport and pitch camp out of sight of these delicate lakelets so other visitors won't find tents in their scenery.

Few hikers to Divide Lake will be able to resist continuing 0.8 mile up the trail to the actual divide — a pass with a view down the forested eastern slope of the Diamond Peak Wilderness. The Pacific Crest Trail is a few hundred yards down the far side, but that hiker byway offers no better views.

Other Hiking Options

Vivian Lake (Hike #95) is 2.9 miles downhill from the trail junction near Notch Lake. A more satisfying side trip, however, is to climb Hemlock Butte for its panoramic view. Return to your car and drive 200 yards back on Road 23 to a hiker-symbol sign at the pass. A half-mile trail here climbs 500 feet to a former lookout tower site atop this rocky knob.

100   Sawtooth Mountain

Easy (around Indigo Lake)
4.8 miles round-trip
600 feet elevation gain
Open late June through October
Map: Cowhorn Mtn. (USGS)

Difficult (to summit)
9.7-mile loop
2200 feet elevation gain
Open mid-July through October

Sawtooth Mountain rises like a 1000-foot wall above Indigo Lake, arguably the prettiest pool in this portion of the Cascades. For an easy hike, stroll around the lake past the base of the cliffs. For a more challenging trek, hike up Sawtooth Mountain itself. The final pitch is trailless, but no technical climbing skills are required and the view stretches from Mt. Jefferson to the Crater Lake rim.

Turn off Highway 58 at the sign for Hills Creek Reservoir 1.3 miles east of Oakridge. After half a mile bear right onto Road 21 and follow this paved route 31.2 miles. Three miles beyond Indigo Springs Campground turn left onto Timpanogas Road 2154 and follow signs for Timpanogas Lake 9.3 miles to Timpanogas Campground, where a hiker-symbol sign points to the trailhead.

The Indigo Lake Trail switchbacks up through a forest of mountain hemlock and true fir for 0.7 mile to a 4-way trail junction. Keep left, following the "Indigo Lake" pointer. In another 1.2 miles, by a pond, the trail to Sawtooth Mountain takes off to the left. Ignore this for the moment and continue straight to a primitive campground on the lakeshore. The site has a picnic table and an outhouse. A sandy beach invites splashing, although the lake bottom is muddy. The lake's indigo coloring is at the far end, where it's deeper. To see it, take the 1-mile shoreline loop.

If you're headed for the summit of Sawtooth Mountain, take the side trail at the pond a few yards before Indigo Lake. This path climbs steadily 1.7 miles,

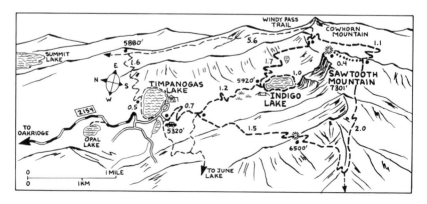

Sawtooth Mountain from Indigo Lake.   Opposite: Indigo Lake from Sawtooth Mountain.

passing a smaller lake in a high meadow and cresting at a high pass. Turn right at a junction just beyond the pass and follow a fainter trail 1.1 miles. This path dips into a valley and then switchbacks up to a sharp ridgecrest with a view of Sawtooth Mountain's cliffs. The official trail turns left at this ridgecrest and begins to descend through the woods, but don't follow it. Instead bushwhack straight up the ridge 0.4 mile. Just before Sawtooth Mountain's summit you'll cross a narrow hogback to a rockslide of clattering, shaley andesite. Don't try to scale the final 10-foot cliff head-on; walk around to the left and hike up the more gradual north face.

To the east is Cowhorn Mountain, named for a spire that fell off in 1911. Below are Indigo, Timpanogas, and Summit Lakes. Timpanogos was an early name for Utah's Great Salt Lake, which an 1830 geographer supposed to be the source of the Willamette River. When the Forest Service later identified that river's origin with more precision, the name was adapted for use here.

To complete the loop, scramble 0.4 mile back to the trail and turn right. This return path is a bit faint, so watch for tree blazes when in doubt.

Other Hiking Options

For a spectacular 11.3-mile loop, return from Indigo Lake via Cowhorn Mountain instead. From the junction just before Indigo Lake, climb 1.7 miles to the pass beside Sawtooth Mountain, but then turn *left* on the Windy Pass Trail. After 2 miles, this well-graded alpine path curves left on the flank of Cowhorn Mountain. (This portion of the map is not to scale.) Follow the trail as it gradually descends another 3.6 miles. Then turn left on a switchbacking 1.6-mile path down to Timpanogas Lake. To complete the loop, turn right along the lakeshore path 0.5 mile to the campground and your car.

100 More Hikes in the Central Oregon Cascades

Adventurous hikers can discover plenty of additional trails in the mountains between Bend and the Willamette Valley. The list below covers the most interesting — from easy, paved nature trails to rugged, faint wilderness paths. Directions are brief, so be extra careful to bring appropriate maps. Note that hikes described as Wilderness pass through areas with special restrictions, particularly for backpackers. Estimated mileages are one-way. Unless noted, snow closes these trails 6 to 9 months of the year. For more information, check with the trail's administrative agency. The appropriate ranger district offices are abbreviated as follows: (B)–Bend, (BR)–Blue River, (C)–Crescent, (CG)–Cottage Grove, (CR)–Crooked River Grasslands, (D)–Detroit, (FR)–Ft Rock, (L)–Lowell, (M)–McKenzie, (O)–Oakridge, (R)–Rigdon, (S)–Sisters, (SH)–Sweet Home.

SANTIAM FOOTHILLS

Whetstone Mountain. Strenuous 5.5-mi climb up 3000 ft to lookout site. Bull of the Woods Wilderness. Park as for Opal Cr (#4). (D)

Mt. Beachie. Pleasant 2.5-mi climb to view of Mt Jefferson, Opal Cr Valley. Wilderness. Gains 800 ft. Park as for Battle Ax (#6). (D)

Stahlman Point. Convenient 2.5-mi climb to lookout site above Detroit Reservoir. Gains 1300 ft. Open mid-Mar to Dec. Drive 2.5 mi E of Detroit on Hwy 22, turn right on Rd 10 for 3.5 mi. (D)

Daly Lake. Level 1.1-mi stroll around woodsy lake. Drive 7.5 mi N of Santiam Y jct on Hwy 22, turn W on Rd 2266 for 5 mi, turn right on Rd 450 for 0.3 mi. (SH)

Donaca Lake. Remote 5-mi hike through old-growth of Middle Santiam Wilderness. Backpackable. At Mountain House Restaurant (23 mi E of Sweet Home) turn N off Hwy 20 onto Rd 2041 for 12.5 mi. (SH)

Heart Lake. Steep, unmaintained 1-mile route to campable lake. 1-mi extension planned to Browder Ridge (#12). At Tombstone Pass, turn off Hwy 20 onto Rd 060 for 3.3 mi to a ridge-end. Unsigned. (SH)

House Rock. 0.8-mile loop at House Rock C G (25 mi E of Sweet Home on Hwy 20) crosses S Santiam R to rock monolith and waterfall, returns via old Santiam Wagon Rd. Open Mar through Dec. (SH)

Gordon Lakes. Downhill, 0.4-mi path to 2 lakes popular with children. Path continues 3.2 mi to Gordon Meadows. Turn S off Hwy 22 at House Rock C G, follow Rd 2044 for 5.5 mi, turn right onto Rd 230 for 2.6 mi to road's end. (SH)

Falls Creek. Woodsy 4.3-mi climb, partly along creek, to Gordon Meadows. Gains 1000 ft. Trail continues to Gordon Lks (see above). Turn S off Hwy 22 at river bridge 16 mi E of Sweet Home, follow Rd 2032 for 5 mi. (SH)

Easy
Moderate
Difficult

MOUNT JEFFERSON

Firecamp Lakes. Gradual 1.2-mi climb through woods to Crown Lake. Drive Rd 46 from Detroit 11.5 mi, turn right on Rd 4685 for 8.3 mi to its end. Wilderness. (D)

Bear Point. Envigorating 3.8-mi climb to lookout site with grand view of Mt Jefferson. Gains 3000 ft. Drive Rd 46 from Detroit 11.5 mi, turn right on Rd 4685 for 5 mi. Wilderness. (D)

Jeff Park via South Breitenbush. Quietest route to this Wilderness mecca. Gains 2800 ft in 6.2 mi. Same trailhead as Bear Pt. (D)

Woodpecker Ridge. 2-mi alpine romp to PCT on shoulder of Mt Jefferson. Views. Wilderness. Drive 11.7 mi E of Detroit on Hwy 22, turn left on Rd 040 for 5 mi to its end. (D)

Hunts Cove. Gorgeous 15.9-mi alpine loop suitable for backpack. Hike to Pamelia L (#20), continue past Hunts Cove to Cathedral Rocks, turn left on PCT 4.8 mi around base of Mt Jefferson, turn left to Pamelia L. Gains 3000 ft. Heavily used portion of Wilderness. (D)

Independence Rock. Convenient 1-mi path to cliff overlooking N Santiam area. Gains 300 ft. Turn off Hwy 22 at Marion Forks, park along Rd 2255 after 100 yds. (D)

Eight Lakes Basin. Backpackable 15.2-mi loop to wildflower meadows, crowded Wilderness lakes. Hike to Marion L (#21), turn right on Blue L Trail 4 mi to Jorn L, turn left to return to Marion L. Gains 1800 ft. (D)

Maxwell Butte. Panoramic viewpoint in Mt Jefferson Wilderness. 4.8-mi trail passes swimmable Twin Lks, gains 2500 ft. Drive 2.5 mi N of Santiam Y jct on Hwy 22, park at Maxwell sno-park. (D)

Washington Meadows. 5.5-mi section of PCT climbs 1300 ft to a viewpoint below Mt Washington's spire. Wilderness. From Santiam Pass, follow signs S to Big Lake, then left to Pacific Crest Trailhead. (M)

Circle Lake. Level 3.3-mi walk via North Blow-Out Shelter to lake with view. On network of stump-filled cross-country ski trails from Benson sno-park. Drive 2 mi S of Santiam Pass on Big Lake Rd 2690. (M)

Blue Lake. 4.5-mile loop through Corbett State Park beside deep, blue lake. Park at sno-park 4.3 mi E of Santiam Pass; trail begins behind restroom, drops 600 ft in 1.3 mi to lake loop. (S)

Suttle Lake. Level 3.7-mi loop around popular lake passes lodge, 3 campgrounds. Drive 7 mi E of Santiam Pass on Hwy 22. (S)

Round and Square Lakes. Fairly flat 2.2-mi Wilderness path from Round L passes Long L, joins Hike #24 at Square L. Drive E of Santiam Pass 8 mi, turn N on Rd 12 for 2.8 mi, turn left on Rd 1210 for 5 mi. (S)

Head of Jack Creek. 0.3-mi loop to massive springs, less well known than Head of Metolius. Drive 8 mi E of Santiam Pass, turn N on Rd 12 to end of pavement, continue straight, follow signs 2 mi. (S)

Table Lake. Challenging, remote 22-mi Wilderness backpack loop up Jefferson Cr Trail and down Sugarpine Ridge. Wildflowers, lava, views of Mt Jefferson. Drive 8 mi E of Santiam Pass, turn N on Rd 12 for 13 mi, turn left on Rd 1292 to its end in 3 mi. (S)

● **Metolius Breaks.** Remote 1.5-mi path along lower Metolius R. Drive W from Hwy 97 through Cove Palisades Park and Grandview to end of Rd 64. (S)

●● **Green Ridge.** Hikable 9.5-mi horse trail up wooded ridge with view of Mt Jefferson. Turn back whenever tired. Drive 5.5 mi W of Sisters on Hwy 20, turn right 4.4 mi on Rd 11, go straight 1.2 mi on Rd 1120. (S)

BEND AREA

● **Tumalo Meadow.** 3.8-mi climb past falls, meadows to N Fk Tumalo Cr. From Tumalo Falls trailhead (#33), hike up Bridge Cr 1.2 mi, turn right. Gains 1100 ft. (B)

● **Lava Butte Nature Trail.** Paved 0.5-mi loop through lava beds explains natural history. Park at Lava Lands Visitor Center 10 mi S of Bend on Hwy 97. Open all year. (FR)

● **Lava River Cave.** 1-mi path through spectacular lava tube. Open all year. Bring lamps, coats. 11.5 mi S of Bend on Hwy 97. (Oregon State Parks)

● **Lava Cast Forest.** Paved 1-mi nature trail explains how lava flow engulfed forest, left interesting casts. Drive 14 mi S of Bend on Hwy 97, turn left on Rd 9720 for 9.5 mi to road's end. (FR)

● **Paulina Peak.** Dusty 2-mi path climbs 1500 ft to breathtaking view of Newberry Crater and Central Oregon. Drive to Paulina Lake (#37), but turn right before toll booth onto Rd 500 for 1 mi to trailhead. Since Rd 500 continues to the summit, trail can also be hiked one-way, downhill. (FR)

● **Big Obsidian Lava Flow.** Paved 0.7-mi nature trail up glassy obsidian lava in Newberry Crater. Fragile area — please stay on trail. Drive to Paulina L (#37), but continue 2.3 mi past toll booth on Rd 21. (FR)

● **The Dome.** 0.7-mi path to cinder cone rim overlooking East L, Ft Rock, high desert. Drive to Paulina L (#37), but continue 7.4 mi past toll booth on Rd 21. (FR)

● **Squaw Creek Canyon.** Trailless route through high desert gorge. Drive 4.5 mi E of Sisters on Hwy 126, turn left on Goodrich Rd 8 mi, turn left on Rd 6360 for 3.4 mi, turn right on Rd 6370 for 0.8 mi, park at gate. Walk 1 mi down rd (keep left at forks), cross creek, scramble up far shore, hike right 1.2 mi to riverbend oasis. Closed Dec 1 to Mar 31. (CR)

● **Fall River.** New 3-mi path follows sparkling, spring-fed stream among old-growth ponderosa pines. Great for kids. Shuttle possible. Drive 17 mi S of Bend on Hwy 97, turn left 12 mi on Rd 42 to Fall River C G. (B)

THE THREE SISTERS

● **Robinson Lake.** Level 0.5-mi path to swimmable lake. Drive 16 mi E of McKenzie Br on Hwy 126, turn right onto Rd 2664 for 4.7 mi to road's end. (M)

● **Dee Wright Observatory.** Paved 0.5-mi nature loop through lava begins at viewpoint atop McKenzie Pass on Hwy 242. (M)

Paulina Lake and Newberry Crater from Paulina Peak.

Easy
Moderate
Difficult

Linton Meadows. Scenic, crowded 9.1-mi backpacking trail climbs to alpine wildflower fields beside Middle Sister. Husband and Eileen Lks nearby. Hike Obsidian Trail (#42) to PCT, follow PCT 2 mi S, turn right for 1.3 mi. Wilderness. (M)

Dugout Lake. Hike 1-mi jeep track to meadowy lake, continue 0.5 mi up ridge to view of Mt Washington. Drive Hwy 242 W of Sisters 7.5 mi, turn right on Rd 1028 for 0.8 mi, turn left on Rd 1030 for 3.4 mi, park at "Dugout Lake" sign, walk Rd 350. (S)

Scott Pass via Alder Creek. Forested 4-mi trail climbs 1000 ft to alpine pass, S Matthieu L (#47), view of N Sister. Wilderness. Drive 5.7 mi W of Sisters on Hwy 242, turn S on Rd 1018 for 6 mi, turn right on Rd 1026 to its end in 1.2 mi. (S)

Squaw Creek Falls. New 1.5-mi trail to 30-ft falls in Wilderness. Drive S of Sisters 8 mi on Rd 16, turn right on Rd 1514 for 5 mi, turn left on Rd 600 to a T-jct, turn onto Rd 680 about a mile to sign at road's end. (S)

Little Three Creek Lake. Charming, level 3-mi loop to lake below McArthur Rim's cliffs. Park as for Hike #51. (S).

Mount Bachelor. Arduous 2.5-mi trail from Sunrise Lodge gains 2700 ft to picture-postcard view at summit also accessible by chairlift. (B)

Todd Lake. 1.7-mi shore loop begins at walk-in campground; 3-mi cross-country circuit of ridge behind lake yields views, wildflowers. Drive 2 mi E of Mt Bachelor on Cascade Lks Hwy, turn right. (B)

● **Todd Trail.** Scenic 3.8-mi path gains 700 ft from Todd L (see above) to wildflower meadows below Broken Top. Wilderness. (B)

● **Soap Creek.** Little-known 4.2-mi route to meadow below N Sister's craggy face. Wilderness. Hike 2 mi on trail toward Chambers Lks (#49), turn right 100 ft before Soap Cr bridge, follow faint, unmarked path up splashing, flower-banked creek, gaining 1500 ft. (S)

● **Sparks Lake to Lava Lake.** Hikable 11-mi horse path through woods from Soda Creek C G (4 mi E of Mt Bachelor on Cascade Lks Hwy) to Lava Lake Lodge. Some lava. Car shuttle recommended. (B)

● **Lucky Lake.** Woodsy 1.3-mi stroll to Wilderness lake. Trail continues 4.7 mi to Senoj L (see Hike #58). Park at well-marked trailhead 5 mi S of Elk L on Cascade Lks Hwy. (B)

MCKENZIE FOOTHILLS

● **Carpenter Mountain Lookout.** 1-mi path to lookout building atop cliff-edged peak. Huckleberries, panoramic views. Drive 3 mi E of Blue River on Hwy 126, turn N on Rd 15 for 3.5 mi, turn right on Rd 1506 for 7 mi, turn left on Rd 350 for 6 mi to saddle. (BR)

● **Delta Nature Trail.** Interpretive 0.5-mi loop in classic old-growth grove at Delta C G, off Hwy 126, 5 mi E of Blue River. Open all year. (BR)

● **Central McKenzie River Trail.** Follows raging river 6.6 mi amid old-growth woods. Shuttle recommended. Leave vehicle at Trailbridge Dam (13 mi E of McKenzie Br on Hwy 126), then start hike 6 mi W on Hwy 126 at bridge near Boulder Cr. Connects with Hikes #62 and #63. (M)

● **Rainbow Falls Viewpoint.** Nearly level 1-mi path to distant view of massive falls, 3 Sisters. Drive 3 mi E of McKenzie Br on Hwy 126, turn S on Rd 2643 for 6.5 mi to sign. Wilderness. (M)

● **Separation Creek.** Remote Wilderness path descends 800 ft in 3.4 mi to roaring creek in deep woods. Drive 3 mi E of McKenzie Br on Hwy 126, turn S on Rd 2643 for 8 mi, turn right on Rd 480 to its end in 1.5 mi. (M)

● **Lower Olallie Trail.** Downhill 4.5-mi path along wooded ridge loses 1900 ft. Shuttle recommended. Start at Horsepasture Saddle as for Hike #67 but hike to shuttle car at trailhead 5.8 mi down Rd 1993. (M)

● **Olallie Mountain.** Wilderness lookout site overlooking French Pete and 3 Sisters. Gains 1300 ft in 3.5 mi. Drive to Cougar Reservoir, cross dam on Rd 1993, continue 15.4 mi. (BR)

●● **East Fork McKenzie.** 6.5-mi creekside Wilderness path through old-growth woods. Parallels Rd 1993, making car shuttle handy. Drive to Cougar Reservoir, cross dam on Rd 1993 to Echo C G. (BR)

● **Terwilliger Hot Springs.** Heavily used 0.5-mi path to crowded natural hot spring pools in forest canyon. Closed after dark. Drive 4 mi past Cougar Dam on Rd 19 to Rider Cr inlet, look for parked cars. (BR)

● **South Fork McKenzie.** Level 3.7-mi riverside walk through old-growth forest in Wilderness. Drive Rd 19 past Cougar Reservoir to Frissell Crossing C G. (BR)

Mink Lake via Roaring River Ridge. Wilderness backpack route gains only 600 ft in 7.7 mi, passing Blondie L, Corral Flat. Drive as to Chucksney Mtn (#71), but turn E off Rd 19 one-half mi N of Box Canyon C G, follow Rd 1958 for 3.2 mi. (BR, M)

Irish Mountain via Otter Lake. 5.8-mi climb to alpine huckleberry fields on shoulder of peak. View of Waldo L. Gains 2000 ft. Park as for Erma Bell Lks (#72). (O)

Hiyu Ridge to Grasshopper Mountain. Quiet 4-mi ridgetop path through alpine meadows and woods to grassy viewpoint. Gains 1200 ft. Drive 6.5 mi past upper end of Cougar Reservoir on Rd 19, turn right on Rd 1927 for 6.3 mi to Lowell Pass. (BR)

Grasshopper Mountain Shortcut. Refreshing 1.4-mi climb to alpine meadows with mountain views. Gains 1000 ft. Drive Rd 19 from Oakridge 13 mi, turn left on Rd 1926 for 3 mi, turn right on Rd 1927 for 2.1 mi, turn right on Rd 1929 for 5.5 mi. (O)

Fisher Creek. Nearly level 2.3-mi walk along Wilderness creek in ancient forest to stream crossing, where trail steepens. Drive Rd 19 from Oakridge 23.2 mi, turn right 2 mi at hiker symbol. Open Apr to Dec. (O)

WILLAMETTE FOOTHILLS

Jasper Bridge Park. All-year, level 1.5-mi path along Middle Fk Willamette R. From I-5, drive E on Hwy 58 for 5.3 mi, turn left on Jasper Rd 2.7 mi to bridge, walk downstream. (Lane County Parks)

Clark Butte. Convenient 2.7-mi trail up 1300 ft to summit view of Fall Cr Valley. Path crosses 2 roads. Drive 2.5 mi past Fall Cr trailhead (#78) to Clark Cr Group Camp. Hike 0.5 mi on nature trail loop to jct with Clark Butte Trail. Open Mar to Dec. (L)

Johnny Creek Nature Trail. Handicapped-accessible, interpretive 0.7-mi path through old-growth forest. Open all year. Drive 3 mi past Fall Cr trailhead (#78), turn right on Rd 1821 for 0.2 mi. (L)

Gold Point. Scenic 4.3-mi ridgecrest path to lookout site gains 2300 ft. Open Apr to Dec. Drive 5.8 mi past Fall Cr trailhead (#78), turn right on Rd 1825 for 2.7 mi, keep left at junctions for another 0.8 mi. (L)

Saddleblanket Mountain. Viewless, subalpine 1.4-mi stroll from Little Blanket Shelter to unclimbable 80-ft lookout tower. Drive 5.3 mi past Fall Cr trailhead (#78), turn right on Rd 1824 for 6.2 mi, turn left on Rd 142 for 1.1 mi, turn right on Rd 144. (L)

Hardesty Mountain. Arduous 5-mi climb gains 3300 ft through forest to lookout site. Park beside Hwy 58 as for Goodman Cr (#80). (L)

Hardesty Mountain Cutoff. 0.9-mile back route to lookout site gains only 600 ft. Turn S off Hwy 58 between mileposts 24 and 25, follow Rd 2840 for 5.1 mi to pass, turn right on narrow Rd 550 to its end. (L)

South Willamette Trail. Relatively level, all-year 4.8-mi path through forest above Hwy 58. Shuttle recommended. Park 1 car as for Goodman Cr (#80), leave other at Eula Ridge trailhead 3 mi E. (L)

North Sister from upper Soap Creek meadow.

Eula Ridge. Steep, less-used 4-mi route to Hardesty Mtn summit gains 3300 ft. Park on Hwy 58, 3 mi E of trailhead for Hike #80. (L)

Lone Wolf Shelter. 1-mi walk to rustic shelter at meadow; new 1.5-mi extension to Patterson Mtn summit. Drive 5 mi W of Oakridge on Hwy 58, turn S on Rd 5847 for 7.8 mi, turn right on Rd 555 for 0.3 mi. (L)

Flat Creek. Almost within Oakridge, 3.3-mi route climbs 2000 ft to viewpoint atop Dead Mtn. Drive 2 mi E of downtown on Salmon Cr Rd 24, turn left on Rd 2404 for 0.7 mi. Hike 2-mi path to closed Rd 210, keep right on road to summit. Open Mar-Dec. (O)

Larison Rock. Switchbacking 0.3-mi climb to view of Oakridge, High Cascades. Drive 1 mi E of Oakridge on Hwy 58, turn S on Rd 23 for 0.5 mi, fork right on Rd 21 for 1 mi, turn right on Rd 2102 for 4 mi to 2nd hiker sign. Open Apr to Dec. (R)

Tufti Trail. Year-round 0.5-mi path between mossy Hills Cr gorge and Rd 24. Waterfalls, pools. Drive 1.3 mi E of Oakridge on Hwy 58, turn S on Rd 23 for 5.8 mi to bridge on right. (R)

Moon Point. 1.1-mi strol to bluff with sweeping view. Fork of trail descends steeply through old-growth 4 mi to Rd 21. Drive 18.4 mi S of Hwy 58 on Rd 21, turn left on Rd 2129 for 9 mi. (R)

Middle Fork Willamette — Upper Portion. New, very scenic 7-mi segment of riverside trail passes spring, small falls. For shuttle, park 1 car at Indigo Spr C G (30 mi S of Hwy 58 on Rd 21), drive 2nd car 3 mi up Rd 21, go straight on Rd 2153 to river bridge. Open Apr to Dec. (R)

Dome Rock. Picturesque 2.2-mi ridgecrest walk from Little Dome Rk to crag with lookout site. From Hwy 58, drive S past Hills Cr Reservoir 21.5 mi on Rd 21, turn right on Rd 2134 for 12 mi, turn right on Rd 250 for 2.5 mi, turn right on Rd 251 for 2.7 mi. (R)

Layng Creek. Sword ferns line this all-year 1-mi creekside loop at Rujada C G, 20 mi E of Cottage Grove. Take Rd 17 past Disston. (CG)

Marten Creek Trail. Ridgecrest path gains 2400 ft in 4 mi to Marten Spring on Adams Mtn; trails continue 2.3 mi to viewless summit or past Crawfish Shelter for 12.3-mi loop. Drive 3.7 mi past Brice Cr trailhead (#85) to sign 200 yds beyond Lund Park. (CG)

Parker Creek Falls. All-year 0.7-mi path skirts Brice Cr gorge to 2 falls on side creek. Drive 7.2 mi past the trailhead for Hike #85 on Rd 22. (CG)

Fairview Creek. Tumbling stream in wooded canyon accessed by all-year, 1-mi trail from Mineral C G. Drive 15.5 mi E of Cottage Grove to Culp Creek, turn right along Sharps Cr 12 mi. (CG)

WILLAMETTE PASS

Bunchgrass Ridge. Alpine path with view, beargrass meadows. Turn back whenever tired. Leads 6 mi to Big Bunchgrass, 14 mi to Black Mdw (#88). Drive 6.5 mi E of Oakridge on Salmon Cr Rd 24, turn right on Rd 5871 for 2.7 mi, turn left on Rd 2408 for 7.0 mi, turn right on unmarked spur 0.3 mi to trailhead at Little Bunchgrass lookout site. (O)

Koch Mountain. Nearly level 2-mile shortcut to remote W shore of Waldo L. Drive 13.5 mi E of Oakridge on Salmon Cr Rd 24, turn left on Rd 2422 for 13.7 mi. Wilderness. (O)

Swan and Gander Lakes. Downhill, 1.2-mi path to Wilderness lakes. Or continue on an 8.8-mi loop to Waldo Mtn lookout (#90). Drive 11 mi E of Oakridge on Salmon Cr Rd 24, fork left on Rd 2417 for 7.2 mi. (O)

Blair Lake to Mule Mountain. Gradual 4.5-mi climb through alpine meadows. Drive 9 mi E of Oakridge on Salmon Cr Rd 24, turn left on Rd 1934 for 8 mi, turn right on Rd 733 for 1.3 mi to Blair Lake C G. (O)

Lily Lake. Woodsy 2.3-mi stroll via PCT from Charlton L down to Lily L. Optional return loop around Charlton Butte. 3 mi W of Willamette Pass, turn N on Rd 5897 for 11.8 mi, turn right on Rd 4290 for 1 mi. (B)

Waldo Lake Loop. Backpackable 20.2-mi circuit of huge alpine lake's shore. Shortcuts possible only with a boat. Park as for #88 or #92. (O)

Bobby Lake. Level 2-mi stroll to large lake. Good hike for kids. 3 mi W of Willamette Pass, turn N on Rd 5897 for 5.5 mi. (O)

Maiden Peak. Rigorous 5.8-mi climb gains 2900 ft to sweeping summit view. 1 mi W of Willamette Pass, turn N on Rd 500 for 1.5 mi. (O)

Marilyn Lakes. Very easy 1.7-mi loop to 2 cute lakes. 1 mi W of Willamette Pass, turn N on Rd 500 for 2 mi to Gold Lake C G, hike 1 mi on trail, 0.7 mi back on Rd 500. (O)

Diamond View Lake. Pleasant 5.4-mi path up Trapper Cr gains 1000 ft to Wilderness source of Whitefish Cr. Start as for Yoran L (#96), turn left at first trail junction. (C)

Oldenburg Lake. Forested 5.2-mi path passes Pinewan and Bingham Lks. Drive to W end of Crescent L on Rd 60. (C)

Effie Lake. Dozens of Wilderness lakelets line this 2.8-mi path. Gains just 400 ft. Park as for Windy Lks (#98) but hike N. (C)

Diamond Peak Shoulder. Hike PCT above timberline to wildflowers, views, spring at head of Mountain Cr. Gains 1400 ft in 6 mi. Park at Emigrant Pass by Summit L on dirt Rd 6010. Access is either via Crescent L (see #98) or Oakridge (take Rd 21). Wilderness. (R)

Marie Lake. Charming meadow-fringed lake with view of Diamond Pk. Route gains 600 ft in 3.3 mi. Park as for Diamond Pk Shoulder (above), hike PCT 2.7 mi N, turn left. Wilderness. (R)

Cowhorn Mountain. Hike Windy Pass Trail 5 mi, passing 3 small lakes, then scramble up trailless, open slope to summit viewpoint. Gains 2000 ft. Drive as to Sawtooth Mtn (#100), but 2 mi before Timpanogas L, turn E on Rd 372 for 0.5 mi. (R)

June Lake. Pleasant 2.3-mi path to lake crosses ridge with view of Mt Thielsen, Hills Pk. Gains 300 ft. Park as for Sawtooth Mtn (#100). (R)

Diamond Peak Loop. Dramatic 29-mile backpack trail around Wilderness mountain. Hike to Divide L (#99), take PCT to S, keep right past Marie and Corrigan Lks. (R,C)

Index

About the Author

A native of Oregon, William L. Sullivan began hiking at the age of 5 and has been exploring new trails ever since. At 17 he left high school to study at remote Deep Springs College in the California desert. He went on to earn a B.A. in English from Cornell University and an M.A. in German from the University of Oregon. He and his wife Janell Sorensen bicycled 3000 miles through Europe, studied at Heidelberg University, and built a log cabin by hand on Oregon's Siletz River.

In 1985 Sullivan set out to investigate Oregon's wilderness by backpacking 1,300 miles from the state's westernmost shore at Cape Blanco to Oregon's easternmost point in Hells Canyon. His journal of that adventure, published as *Listening for Coyote,* was a finalist for the Oregon Book Award in creative nonfiction. Since then he has authored *Exploring Oregon's Wild Areas* and a series of *100 Hikes* guidebooks to the regions of Oregon. He and Janell live in Eugene with their children Karen and Ian.